PENGUIN BOOKS
2406

THE HOUSE THAT NINO BUILT

Giovanni Guareschi still lives at Parma, near the River Po, where he was born in 1909. His parents wished him to be a naval engineer: consequently he studied law, made a name as a sign-board painter, and, among other jobs, gave mandolin lessons. His father had a heavy black moustache under his nose: Giovanni grew one just like it. He still has it and is proud of it. He is not bald, has written eight books, and is five feet ten inches tall. 'I also have a brother,' Guareschi says, adding, 'but I prefer not to discuss him. And I have a motor-cycle with four cylinders, an automobile with six cylinders, and a wife and two children.'

As a young man he drew cartoons for *Bartoldo*. When the war came he was arrested by the political police for howling in the streets all one night. In 1943 he was captured by the Germans at Alessandria and adopted the slogan: 'I will not die even if they kill me.' Back in Italy after the war he became editor-in-chief of *Candido* at Milan in which his famous *Don Camillo* stories first appeared. He has also scripted a film, *People Like This*.

GIOVANNI GUARESCHI

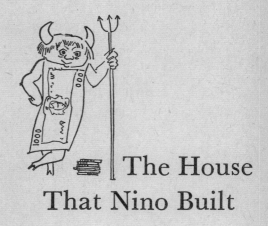

The House
That Nino Built

Translated from the Italian
by Frances Frenaye

PENGUIN BOOKS

Penguin Books Ltd, Harmondsworth, Middlesex, England
Penguin Books Australia Ltd, Ringwood, Victoria, Australia

This translation first published in the U.S.A. 1953
Published in Great Britain by Victor Gollancz 1953
Published in Penguin Books 1967
Copyright © Giovanni Guareschi, 1953

Made and printed in Great Britain by
C. Nicholls & Company Ltd
Set in Monotype Baskerville

This book is sold subject to the condition that
it shall not, by way of trade or otherwise, be lent,
re-sold, hired out, or otherwise circulated without
the publisher's prior consent in any form of
binding or cover other than that in which it is
published and without a similar condition
including this condition being imposed on the
subsequent purchaser

Contents

A Frail Ship on the High Seas

As I see it, the Good Lord, when He drove Adam out of the Garden of Eden, didn't simply tell him that he would have to earn his bread with the sweat of his brow. As I see it, the Good Lord must have also roared, 'And your wife will economize.' Otherwise it is impossible to explain how this sense of economy, which women possess among many other important defects, becomes such a torment to all husbands.

Here is what I mean. One evening we are sitting at the table. We – that is a young lady who was baptized Carlotta but for reasons that will become clear later is always called the Duchess, Albertino who was baptized Albertino and in the brief years since then has determinedly stuck to it, Margherita who is the author of the two aforesaid individuals and is related to me in one way or another.

When supper was over, the Duchess turned off the radio. I told her to leave it on, because the programme was one I wanted to hear.

'Later on,' she told me. 'First we have to hold our meeting.'

'A meeting? What do you mean? Isn't that something new?'

'It's not new,' said Margherita, coming up with pens and notebooks. 'We hold a meeting every night now, after supper. It's something we started while you were away.'

She sat down, opened a notebook and proceeded to explain further.

'Every meeting has two parts. First, drawing up a balance sheet of the twenty-four hours that have just gone by; second, staking out a budget of the twenty-four that are to follow.'

I confessed that although it was all crystal-clear, I didn't understand a word of it. Very patiently, Margherita gave me the details.

'Until a very short time ago, we lived like a family of horses, grazing in the fields and taking what comes without thought for the morrow. We've never had any organization, and an unorganized family is like a house without a foundation; it holds up as long as it can, but no one can guarantee its stability. Now we're living according to plan, and that's an extremely important thing. Because when the children take part in a discussion of this kind they learn to run a family and to distinguish between essentials and superfluities. Instead of growing up in cotton-wool, they acquire an idea of the difficulties they're sure to run up against later.'

I was overcome with admiration.

'The children have caught on already to the basic idea,' said Margherita. 'Duchess, give your father a definition of the family from an organizational point of view.'

The Duchess recited in a single breath:

'From an organizational point of view, the family is like a ship, with the father pulling the oars, the mother at the helm and the children helping them out in order that they, in their turn, may be rowers and pilots one day. Amen.'

'This is no time for joking,' Margherita said reproachfully. 'Let's get started. Has anyone something to say about the management of the last twenty-four hours? Was all our money spent well?'

Albertino and the Duchess looked at one another.

'As far as I'm concerned, it was,' said Albertino.

'I didn't approve of spending it on chicken soup,' said the Duchess. 'Spaghetti would have suited me better.'

Margherita shook her head.

8

'After you've boiled a chicken, you have to use the water in which it was cooked for chicken soup. . . . Anything else to say? Was there anything we could have done without?'

'Yes,' mumbled the Duchess. 'The salt you poured into the soup, after Giacomina had seasoned it in the kitchen. It was awful.'

Margherita did not respond to this provocation.

'Let's start on the budget for tomorrow,' she said. 'Remember that your father's with us. Write it down, Duchess.'

The Duchess gritted her teeth, dipped her pen into the ink and wrote at the top of a new page: '*Thursday, March 5 – Members enrolled: 5; Members present: 5.*' Then she read aloud what she had just written.

'Good,' said Margherita in a clipped, almost military manner. 'Now, Albertino, call the roll of our commissary *units.*'

'Five units of bread for breakfast, five for lunch, two for tea and five for supper. Total, seventeen units.'

'Sixteen,' said the Duchess. 'I want a unit of cornmeal for supper.'

'Thumbs down on that,' said Margherita. 'Impractical and uneconomic. It has to be a hundred per cent bread or a hundred per cent cornmeal, one or the other.'

So five units of cornmeal were approved for supper.

'Every *unit,* whether it's of bread or anything else, is tied up with its weight and cost,' Margherita explained to me. 'We have a reference manual right at hand.'

After agreement had been reached on the soup and main course for lunch, the board of directors set the number of units required.

'We need a unit of pork liver for the cat,' said the Duchess.

'The cat doesn't count,' said Margherita. 'He'll have to make do with the leftovers. Now, let's add up our figures. How much are we spending for food tomorrow?'

Albertino and the Duchess worked for some time over the addition, but the sum they obtained did not please Margherita. They did it over and got a very different result, but still their mother was not satisfied. Then Giacomina stepped in, and the figures came out right. But Margherita shook her head.

'It comes to two hundred liras over what it was today. That won't do. Tomorrow we must plan more carefully. Meanwhile, since we have to balance both sides of the ledger, we'll take the two hundred liras out of the funds allotted to *Group B*.'

This required some explanation for my benefit.

'We budgeted the amount we're supposed to spend during the year on wearing apparel, shoes, washing, ironing, shoe repairs, mending, light, heat, bottled gas, servants, amusements, travel, cigarettes, school, cultural pursuits, postage stamps, medicine, house repairs, summer vacation, amortization of capital, etc., etc. Then, after we added this all up we divided it by 365, in order to see how much we are entitled to spend every day. All these things come under *Group B*. *Group B* is in another notebook, broken down alphabetically.'

After I had leafed through *Group B*, I was lost in amazement.

'Did you set this up, Margherita?' I asked her.

'No, it was set up by Signora Marcella, on the basis of her family, which is just the same size as ours. Of course, she took our tenor of life into account. It's a model of exactitude. You can be sure that under approximately normal conditions, such as those of today, household expenses come to just so much.'

I looked at the figure to which she was pointing, and found it staggering.

'Margherita!' I stammered. 'I can't afford to spend that amount every day.'

'I understand, Nino,' Margherita said with a smile. 'You're reasoning like an automobile owner who says: "My car does twenty-five miles to a gallon. And since a gallon costs twenty-five cents, it costs me a cent a mile to run." But what about oil, and tyres and repairs and taxes and insurance? Just put that in your pipe, Giovannino, and smoke it!'

I inhaled deeply and saw that Margherita was right. But the knowledge filled me with dismay.

'It's terrifying, Margherita,' I panted.

The Duchess intervened.

'Giacomina!' she called. 'A unit of brandy!'

Giacomina brought me the brandy and I gulped down a glass of it on the spot.

'Have some more, if you like, Giovannino,' said Margherita reassuringly. 'It'll come out of the emergency fund.'

The brandy bucked me up and I examined the *Group B* lists. Everything was deadly accurate, and I realized that each day of my life cost me a frightening amount of money. I hadn't ever thought of it in these terms before, but now I felt the weight of it on my shoulders.

'Margherita,' I said, 'from an organizational point of view, the family is like a ship, with the father pulling the oars, the mother at the helm and the children helping them out in order that they in their turn may be rowers and pilots one day. That's a splendid definition. But if every time the rower dips his oar he has to think of the disturbance he is creating in the ocean, the number of calories he is consuming, the amount of oxygen he has breathed in, the quantity of his red blood corpuscles, the variations of his nervous tension, vitamins, proteins, toxins, the gradual decalcification of his tibia, the twinges of his sciatic nerve, his blood pressure, his absorption of ultra-violet rays, the contractions of his stomach, etc., etc., etc. . . . Well, Margherita, do you know what this poor rower will eventually do?'

'Jump into the water!' said the Duchess grimly, going straight to the heart of the matter.

'Yes, jump into the water and drown. That is, after figuring out the exact amount of liquid displaced by his body.'

Margherita threw out her arms.

'Nino, you mustn't be like an ostrich that hides its head in the sand in order to avoid the sight of anything unpleasant. We've got to live with *awareness* of what we are doing. And we can only achieve this awareness through relentless organization.'

But I didn't agree.

'Margherita,' I said, 'there's only one sort of family organization that's bearable to me. The father rows quietly and happily along, drinking in the joy of navigating through so vast a sea; while the children watch him and learn from his example that navigation requires ceaseless rowing.'

'What about the mother?' asked Albertino. 'What does she do?'

'The mother tries not to bother her husband and children,' said the Duchess.

Margherita withered her with a glance. Then she poured herself a unit of brandy and dumped the *Group A* and *Group B* notebooks into the fire.

'The mother removes her irksome presence from the scene,' she said as she got up. 'She relinquishes the helm and retires.'

'*Members enrolled: 5; Members present: 4,*' mumbled the Duchess. '*Members in bed until eleven o'clock tomorrow morning: 1.*'

Margherita disappeared, and the abandoned ship sank, with all its crew, in the enormous fruit tart which Giacomina had brought to the table under the pretext of a *drastic emergency*.

Odyssey of a Counterfeit

THE next day I went to the centre of the town to do some errands, and when I had finished I found myself with a thousand-lira note in my wallet and no cigarettes. I walked into the cigar store, threw my thousand-lira note on the counter and asked for a packet of Luckies.

'What's that?' the man asked, looking with curiosity at the banknote.

'A thousand-lira note,' I answered.

He called his wife, who was reading a newspaper at the back of the shop.

'Look at this, Maria,' he said.

She turned her head around and peered at it from afar.

'Oh, so it's come back to the centre of town,' she observed.

The tobacconist asked me if I lived in the section of Porta Volta.

'No, I live near Lambrate,' I explained.

'Then it's changed its beat again,' he said. 'It hasn't been around here for a whole month. We all know it very well.'

I looked at the banknote myself and gasped. It was without a doubt the falsest piece of paper of its kind in the whole universe. So shamelessly false as to be positively disgusting. Even the manufacture of counterfeit money requires a certain amount of professional dignity. A counterfeiter has to respect the shape of the banknote in question, and as for the design, even if he can't achieve an exact copy he must

13

try to make a passable imitation. Whereas the specimen lying on the counter before me was a completely arbitrary version. A thousand-lira note of this kind could hardly expect to be valued at anything more than fifty liras. I handed back the cigarettes and pocketed the money.

'Too bad you couldn't get away with it,' the tobacconist sneered. 'Well, the way life is, you have to take things as they come.'

I had to go all the way home on foot, and I arrived in anything but a happy frame of mind.

'Did everything go all right?' Margherita asked.

'Right as rain,' I answered, ashamed to confess that I had accepted a counterfeit.

'Splendid!' said Margherita, 'Then you must have passed off that beastly counterfeit thousand-lira note that I slipped into your wallet.'

I am not speaking to young blades, but to seasoned men, to veterans of matrimony. They know that women are adepts at tricks of this kind. Among well-brought-up girls the notion that a husband is something of a guinea-pig is extremely common. I needn't go into this subject any farther. In any case, I kept my feelings under control. I took the cursed note out of my pocket and handed it to Margherita, saying, 'If you're naïve enough to be taken in by such a horror then you must accept the consequences. The thing to do is to throw it into the fire. First of all it's a crime to put counterfeit money into circulation. You can read that on the note itself, in the upper right and left-hand corners.'

In the right and left-hand corners Margherita could see nothing but an array of undecipherable dots and dashes. After all, no one could expect a counterfeit note to extol the law. But even when she was faced with the statements on an authentic note Margherita did not change her mind.

'Whoever gave it to me will have to take it back, that's all,' she said baldly.

'And who did give it to you, Margherita?'

'I don't know. I buy food in so many different places that it might be almost anyone.'

She went out and came back after two hours, which was pretty soon when you come to think of it. To pick a fight with a baker, a butcher, a grocer, a shoemaker, a tobacconist, a dressmaker and a pushcart peddler takes some time. Even if she could pick a fight in two minutes flat, as most of the fair sex can, it was something of a record. Meanwhile Margherita brought the note back with her, more counterfeit than ever.

In a case like this the superintendent's wife is invaluable. She came up to our apartment and Margherita put it up to her squarely.

'If you can get rid of it we'll go halves.'

Two gloomy days went by until the superintendent's wife brought Margherita a handsome five-hundred lira note.

'I had to take it to another part of town,' she explained. 'In the shops around here everybody knew it, even the delivery boys. Now it can go where it sees fit.'

I have already said that the falsity of the note was shameless and disgusting. There was something ugly and arrogant about it and we were glad to have it gone. The whole street seemed to be relieved, because this note was the terror of all the shopkeepers and their customers as well. But one day the superintendent's wife came upstairs with a dire warning.

'It's back!' she announced. 'An old woman just tried to pass it off in the delicatessen.'

In the course of the following days the note turned up again at the grocer's, the butcher's and the shoemaker's, and there was increasing nervousness on both sides of the street. Then suddenly no one spoke of it any more, for the main and simple reason that it was in Margherita's handbag. When we first discovered it there we looked at one another in dismay. Then, to cut matters short, I took it and started to hold it over the gas burner. But Margherita was on the alert and captured it in mid-air.

'It's a question of principle,' she said harshly. 'I took it and I'll get rid of it.'

The next few days were painful for all of us. Margherita covered the whole city and came back at night completely worn out. Finally she gave in and called the wife of the superintendent.

'See what you can do,' she said. 'We'll go halves on it.'

The whole street was upset again, because the superintendent's wife took vigorous action and enlisted the aid of all the cooks of the neighbourhood. Then peace and quiet returned once more. A week later the superintendent's wife handed Margherita a brand new five-hundred lira note.

'I did it,' she said. 'But I had to go as far as Baggio. However, now that it's out in the suburbs we needn't worry.'

Margherita has strange notions of arithmetic and that evening she seemed very pleased with herself.

'Giovannino,' she said. 'Now we've broken even. I got five hundred liras the first time and five hundred the second. So a thousand liras have gone out and a thousand liras have come in.'

I did not raise any objections, and so we went peacefully to bed. But at one o'clock in the morning Margherita woke up with a start.

'Giovannino!' she exclaimed. 'If I were to get back the counterfeit note and make the same deal with the superintendent's wife I could make another five hundred liras. How do you explain that?'

'Better forget about it,' I answered.

Margherita did forget about it for four whole weeks. Then one evening I heard a dreadful cry from the kitchen. I ran in and found Margherita looking with horror-stricken eyes into a drawer in the cupboard. And of course in the drawer lay the famous thousand-lira note. This time I did not hesitate. Grasping it with a pair of pincers, because the very touch of it was disgusting, I started to hold it over the gas. Margherita offered no opposition, but just at the crucial moment the gas went out. Margherita groaned and sank into a chair.

Naturally, it was pure chance that brought about a failure of the gas just as its flames were about to devour a thousand-lira note as false as Judas. Any reasonable man would have a good laugh, then light a match and carry out his original intention. But instead I put the note back in the drawer.

You have every right not to believe a story like this, which contains so much supernatural rubbish. Such things are so stupid that it's a shame to waste time talking about them.

You are quite within your rights but facts are facts all the same. This chain of events obsessed us, and every now and then we opened the drawer and peered at the diabolical thousand-lira note. It was as ugly and arrogant as ever, and so false that you could see through it even when the drawer was closed.

One day I told the whole story to a friend of mine who is a bank teller. He asked to see the note, so we put it in an envelope and took it over. Margherita shuddered when she saw how carelessly he fingered it and held it up to the light for inspection.

'It's a bad printing job but there's nothing else wrong. We could use plenty more as good as this one.'

Then he tied it up with a wad of its fellows and gave us two five-hundreds in exchange. We could hardly speak all the way home. But at a certain point Margherita came to a halt.

'Giovannino,' she said, 'I got five hundred from the superintendent's wife the first time, five hundred the second and now we've got two five-hundreds more. That makes two thousand. Have we made a thousand liras or haven't we?'

'Anything can happen in the world of today,' I answered.

'Perhaps this story has a philosophical significance that escapes us,' Margherita continued. 'Do you think that something good may dog a man's footsteps to the point of persecution? Where is one to draw the boundary line between good and evil?' The mention of boundary lines caused another thought to flit into Margherita's mind. 'I'd like to go for a trip abroad,' she said suddenly and irrelevantly. 'Austria is calling me. The romantic melancholy of it has got under my skin.'

Vacation from Home

Now, next to machinery, the thing Margherita dislikes most is travelling in foreign lands, and so I felt there was something in the wind besides the call of Austria, romantic or otherwise.

I was sure of it when Margherita said,

'We've seen too much of each other.'

I was reading the paper, and this categorical statement took me by surprise.

'What do you mean?' I asked.

'Just what I said. We've seen too much of each other. Unlike other men, who go to their office every day, you have the kind of job you can do at home. And because I can't very well do my housework anywhere but in the house, we see each other all day long. There's never a break, because even when you're free to go somewhere, you prefer to hang around. Do you think it can go on forever?'

To tell the truth, I'd never thought of it as a problem. Obviously it didn't bother me the way it did Margherita. 'As far as I'm concerned, it can,' I answered. 'Of course there's a more magnificent view from the terrace of a sky-scraper in Genoa. But that doesn't alter the fact that I can look at you without displeasure.'

'Looking is one thing and seeing is another!' Margherita insisted. 'When I look at you, I really do see you as well, but you hardly ever see me at all. You look at me with the eyes of habit, and the eyes of habit don't see.'

Things were getting serious, but I didn't think it advisable to argue. I threw out my arms in resignation and said:

'Well, Margherita, if that's the way it is, what can we do about it?'

'We've seen too much of each other,' Margherita repeated. 'We've got to find a way of seeing each other less.'

'Since my work doesn't call me away, and you must look after the house and send the children to school, I don't see how it can be done. You can always go around blindfolded, of course.'

'What difference would that make?' Margherita exclaimed. 'I'd see you just the same. I've seen you so often that I don't need to look at you any more. I can see you with my eyes closed.'

This gave me a come-back.

'You're admitting that you rely on force of habit, just the way I do!'

'In case of emergency, yes, I do,' said Margherita firmly. 'If I'm blindfolded and can't see you, it's only logical that I should see you with the eyes of habit. But with you, the process is systematic.'

We went thoroughly into the necessity of seeing less of one another, and finally came up with a solution.

Our house has a sort of superstructure which forms its third floor, where years ago I set up a little private three-room apartment of my own, complete with bedroom, bath and study. I had the notion that if I could go up there and get away from it all I'd be able to concentrate on my work. But almost from the start, I found that ideas are refractory to stair-climbing. They stick close to the ground, and the highest they ever get is the second floor. And sometimes, in order to get them this high, I had to go all the way down.

It's a great nuisance, but there you are. We middle-class men pick up our ideas in the kitchen and pantry, in the rooms where our family is living. We haven't the imagination to make something out of nothing. Our ideas must be rooted in reality, and we're lost unless we're in direct contact with the little world in which we live, the world of our home.

So it was that I abandoned my private apartment and came down into the life of the first and second floors, leaving behind me one of those useless collections of books and old newspapers to which we are more attached than if we actually used them every day. Now I was able to say:

'Margherita, I'll settle up on the third floor. My life will be entirely separate from yours. I'll eat and sleep up there and whenever I have to go out, which won't be very often, I'll ring the bell six times so as to give you a chance to take refuge in the pantry or kitchen and not see me go by. As for supplies, you just ring five times and I'll lower a basket down the stair-well to receive them. Then when you ring three times, I'll pull them up to my den.'

Margherita thought this made very good sense, and we agreed to start the next day.

*

It was all very touching. I had packed my belongings in a big suitcase and dressed in travelling clothes.

'Father's going on a trip,' Margherita told the children. 'He's been called away by business and he'll be gone a month or more. Say good-bye and promise you'll behave yourselves.'

I gave the children the customary admonitions.

'If you need anything, call me up or drop me a line,' I said to Margherita.

Then I picked up my suitcase and walked through the pantry towards the stairs.

'Have a good time!' called out Albertino.

Just then the Duchess came along with my umbrella and hung it over my arm. As I thanked her, I thought I caught a glimmer of contempt in her eyes. I went slowly up the stairs, and when I reached the third floor I leaned over to wave at those below. Then I turned the key twice in the lock of my private apartment and began to feel as if I were at least fifty miles from home. It was just nine o'clock. I unpacked my bag, laid my things in the chest of drawers, put on my working clothes and sat down in front of the type-writer. It was wonderfully peaceful up there, and the knowledge that I was considered to be away and no one would ring me up on the telephone or knock at the door gave me an extraordinary feeling of relaxation. I worked very hard, and before I knew it, it was one o'clock.

The bell rang to tell me that lunch was ready, and I went out on the landing, lowered the basket and waited for the signal of: 'Lunch is in the basket; take it away!' The five rings came a few minutes later, but I didn't have time to get up from my chair and go out on the landing, because the Duchess appeared at the door with a tray.

'I've brought it to you,' she said. '*She* thinks I'm in the bathtub. *She's* singing like a lark and you're up here all alone.'

While I was eating she gave me news of everything that had happened during my absence.

'Just pretend I didn't come,' she told me at the end. 'Send the dishes down in the basket. I'll be back later, when the coast is clear.'

I thanked her for having me on her mind. At two o'clock I went back to work and had just started to move full speed ahead when Albertino appeared at the door.

'They've both gone out,' he said, 'and I've brought you a cup of coffee. I hope you like it.'

The coffee was excellent, and while I was drinking it, Albertino told me about everything that had gone on on the lower floors.

'I'll be back later,' he concluded. 'Meanwhile, I must beat it. If they don't find me when they come back they'll know I'm up here.' And just as he was going out of the door he turned around to add:

'If you need anything, roll up a wad of red paper and throw it down into the circular flower-bed. I'll look out there every quarter of an hour, and if I find your message I'll say I'm going to my own room and come here instead.'

'Good,' I answered. 'But remember you'll have to look out every quarter of an hour.'

Then I went back to work and stayed at it for at least forty-five minutes without stopping. Then I heard a noise, looked up and saw Margherita at the door.

'The children are out playing,' she said, 'and I thought I'd bring you a cup of tea.'

I appreciated her thoughtfulness and while I was enjoying the tea, she gave me an account of the events of the day.

'When I'm all alone in such a big house, I must admit it's lonely,' she sighed.

'You've got the children to keep you company,' I answered.

'Poor things!' she said, shaking her head. 'I'm sorry for them. Ever since you went away, they're like two little orphans.'

'How's the weather down there?' I asked sadly.

'Rainy and damp,' she answered. 'It's quite different up here.'

Then she hurried to go downstairs before the children came in.

'Will you be away for long?' she asked me before leaving.

'It all depends on my work,' I answered.

Margherita disappeared and I went back to pouring out my story to the typewriter. Half an hour later, there was a sound at the door and I went to open it. It was the cat, crouching on the landing and looking up at me without saying a word, but with a kindly expression. I packed my suitcase and went down to the ground floor.

'Father's back!' Albertino shouted as soon as he saw me.

'So you had a good trip, did you?' said Margherita with satisfaction in her voice.

'And as usual, you've lost your umbrella,' jeered the Duchess.

The cat made no comment.

It was supper-time by now, and we all sat down at the table.

'*Incipit vita nova!* Tomorrow's another day!' said Margherita joyfully.

Mysteries of the Calendar

A BIRTHDAY, that is, the passage from one year of life to another, is the easiest thing in the world to achieve (barring the untimely decease of the interested party). Time goes by with clocklike regularity, and it's practically impossible to get there either too early or too late since every birthday has a way of arriving just a year after the one that went before and a year before the one that is to follow. In a well-regulated family, that is, one where birthdays have been planned to fall as nearly as possible all together, everything goes on greased wheels. Our family is exceptionally well regulated, and so last time it all went off very smoothly. My birthday is May 1, Margherita's is May 4 and May 14 is Albertino's.

'And what about me?' asked the Red Duchess. 'How come I am the only one in this house that hasn't got a birthday? Wasn't I born like everybody else?'

Margherita was indignant.

'Don't go making insinuations! We're all equals here, and everyone that's born has a birthday. Yours comes round on the 13th of November.'

But the Red Duchess wasn't so easily put off.

'Everyone else has a birthday now. Why do I have to wait until winter? Why are all the rest ahead of me?'

I came in at this point and tried to content her with an elementary explanation.

'A birthday is the anniversary of your birth. If a man was born on February 15, then February 15 will always be his birthday. You can't set your birthday at any date you please. Alberto was born on May 14 and celebrates his birthday on that day; you were born on November 13 and celebrate on the 13th of November. But exactly the same number of days go by for both of you in between.'

The Duchess stared at me mistrustfully.

'You say that because you have a birthday in May, just like the rest of them. But I want to see the figures.'

Only one person in a thousand could have laughed at such a demand, and I happened to be that one. Because every New Year's Eve for the last twenty-five years I have taken down the calendar of the past year, laid it aside and hung up a new one of the kind that leaves enough white space around each day to serve as an engagement pad and reminder as well. So now I went to my study and came back with a pile of old calendars.

'Here you are!' I exclaimed. 'Here's the evidence! If you know how to count, let's see you do it.'

'I know how to count up to 410,' the Duchess answered gloomily.

'That's nothing to brag about,' interpolated Margherita. 'When I was your age, I could count up to 2500.'

'I might be able to go that far too, if I tried,' retorted the Duchess.

'Why don't you try, then?'

'I've never had more than 410 liras,' said the Duchess with all the pride of a poor but honest woman.

I set before her calendars for 1940, 1941, 1943, and 1944.

'There,' I said. 'Since Alberto was born on May 14, 1940, and you were born on November 13, 1943, all you have to do is see whether there is the same number of days between May 14, 1940 and May 14, 1941 on the one hand, and between November 13, 1943 and November 13, 1944 on the other. Every year is just like the one before, so after that you won't have to do any more counting.'

The Duchess asked for a red pencil to mark off the days

and started to work. It took her some time, for she repeated the operation at least three times and then had it checked by a trustworthy person who did not belong to the family. After this, she was ready to state the results.

'After one year he covers 365 days and I cover 366. I knew there was a catch to it somewhere. It's all *her* fault, because she wants to age me fast and see me die before her son.'

Margherita couldn't let this accusation go unanswered.

'Talk about counting up to 410!' she exclaimed. 'You're such a little donkey that you don't even know how to count to 365!'

And she sat down in front of the calendars and started counting out loud: 'One, two, three ...' until she came to the end of Albertino's year with a triumphal '365!' After which she proceeded to reel off the Duchess' first year, only this time her conclusion was not triumphant and she did it all over again.

'I must be nervous,' she proclaimed. 'It's 366! ... What are you up to, Nino? Why does Albertino's first year come to 365 days and the Duchess' to 366? You shouldn't play favourites with your children.'

According to Margherita's logic, the head of the family is always to blame. Even the Duchess looked at me severely.

'There's no favouritism,' I explained resentfully. 'It's simply because 1944 was a leap year!'

'Oh, you and your leap years and diphthongs and syllogisms and all the rest! Are we going back to school? It happens that your daughter's future is at stake. Every year, you rob her of a day of life.'

'Every four years!' I answered promptly. 'And what have I to do with it, anyhow? It's February, which every four years has twenty-nine days instead of twenty-eight.'

The Duchess snickered.

'It's funny that you should have to unload that day on me!'

I protested loudly that I wasn't unloading anything on anybody, and that the father of a family can't be held responsible for the vagaries of the calendar. I took out the encyclopaedia and read the appropriate passage: '*The Romans counted 365 days in the year. But since it takes the earth approximately 365 1/4 days to revolve round the sun, the extra six hours had begun, by the time of Julius Caesar, to be a source of considerable concern . . .*'

But Margherita would not let me go on.

'Oh yes, Julius Caesar, the Roman Empire, the imperial eagles, the marching legions, and so on! Do we have to go into all that? When your daughter complains that you're stealing days out of her life, you can think of nothing better than an apology for the Fascist régime!'

'I'm not apologizing for anything,' I shouted. 'I'm simply proving that leap year is not a creature of my invention, that it's a reality from which nobody can escape.'

'But when a little girl imagines herself to be a victim of injustice, it's no use going into an historical survey of leap year.'

'But there isn't any injustice. Albertino has to reckon with the leap years too.'

'I don't care,' put in the Duchess. 'Just as soon as I was born, you threw a leap year at me.'

When people are in such bad faith, there's no use arguing with them. I dumped all the calendars between 1940 and 1950 on to the table.

'How old was Albertino on May 14, 1950?' I asked.

'Ten,' answered the Red Duchess.

'And how many days are there in ten years?'

Margherita threw up her hands in despair.

'It all depends. If you're speaking of ordinary years, then there are 3650, but if you mean leap years, then there are 3660.'

The Red Duchess shook her head.

'Those long years all come to me,' she said. 'It's no use counting.'

I didn't try to discuss that one.

'Let's get down to something concrete,' I said. 'Let's count the days from May 14, 1940 to May 14, 1950.'

The poor things counted the squares on page after page of the calendars, and finally came up with the sum of 3657.

That is the number of days in eight ordinary years and two leap years, 1944 and 1948.

Then I asked them to count the days from November 13, 1943 to November 13, 1950, and here the result was 2557, that is including five ordinary years and the same two leap years. I was triumphant. The Duchess could see it, and she looked in perplexity at Margherita, who didn't seem to be convinced.

'What of it?' she asked. 'Ten years come to 3657 days and seven years come to 2557. Now we must find the relative value of every year. If we divide 3657 by 10 we find that every one of Albertino's years comes to 365.7 days. While if we divide 2557 by seven it turns out that the Duchess averages only 365.3. So you're taking 4/10 of a day from her every year, and in seven years that means you've robbed her of 2 days, 2 hours and 24 minutes. By the time she's seventy, she'll be about 21 days in the red. That's not the way a father should behave.'

I said her arithmetic must have gone haywire, and that a recount would prove it.

'Work it out for yourself,' Margherita said, giving me a pencil and paper.

I did try to work it out, and all the doubts I had harboured for so long about the multiplication table were suddenly brought to a head, inspired, perhaps, by the implacable spirit of my arithmetic teacher. At one point I found myself face to face with a square root, without the slightest notion of where it had come from. And I realized that, if I went on, I might come up against the kind of equation to which I have never been able to attach even the most allegorical meaning.

'I didn't invent the calendar,' I grumbled, throwing away all my tools. 'You can't hold me responsible for leap years.'

'I'm the one to lose,' sobbed the Duchess. 'I'm the youngest of the family, and everybody takes advantage of me. They unload longer years upon me, and then they rob me of twenty-one days.'

The situation was serious.

'It's a question of social justice,' said Margherita. 'Those twenty-one days are hers, and she ought to have them. We must either move her birthday, or else divide our family celebration into two parts, one on May 13 and the other on the 13th of November.'

At last the Duchess was appeased. Thanks to leap year and Margherita's bright idea, she was compensated for the loss of twenty-one days by a double number of birthdays and all the presents that went with them.

'Under a democratic government,' Margherita concluded, 'these leap years ought to be abolished. They tend to create a privileged class and, as usual, to underline the inferior status of women.'

This was a notable conclusion, and one worthy of scrutiny on the part of our deputies in parliament.

At the Fair

ALL this talk about birthdays makes me think back to a time when the Duchess had had only about five birthdays.

It's quite tiring, under any circumstances, to visit the Industrial Fair. After making the rounds of all the displays, your legs are bound to crumple. And to go with the Duchess was an enterprise of heroic proportions. The Duchess was not one of those silly children that beg for soft drinks and candies or whine because they just can't go a step farther. She carried her tender years with dignity and discretion. She was very self-controlled and excellent company. The only trouble was that she had a weakness for heavy machinery. That is why I rewarded her for her good behaviour by taking her to the Industrial Fair and obtaining a special pass to the exhibit of Fiat motors.

As soon as the Red Duchess saw a piece of machinery over six feet high she would bombard me with questions:

'What's that?'

'A Diesel engine.'

'Why?'

There's the trouble, in a nutshell. *Why* is a Diesel engine? Once this difficulty has been hurdled, there is more to follow.

'What's its name?'

'Who's its father?'

'Where does it live?'

'Is it a good engine or a bad one?'

The Duchess' curiosity is insatiable, and she must know whether a given machine can read and write, the number of its brothers and sisters and so on. She hasn't yet inquired too closely into the matter of morals, but once, in front of a big tractor she shot at me: 'Is that one a Communist?' At which point Margherita cut her short with a brusque:

'Children shouldn't meddle with politics!'

This explains the hazards of taking the Duchess to the Industrial Fair. There was no telling what might attract her attention.

Every now and then, for instance, a loudspeaker announced above the clamour of the crowd: 'Will the parents of such and such a child call at the Information Desk? . . .'

'Why do they want those parents to call?' the Red Duchess asked.

That one was easy.

'Occasionally, some naughty child loses his father and mother, and when he starts bawling his head off, they take him to the Information Desk and notify the parents to call for him there.'

'Do the parents spank him?'

'Of course.'

'Do they spank him very hard?'

'Fairly hard. They box his ears and then turn him over their knees . . .'

'That's very bad of them. They shouldn't hit their children.'

'But children ought to stay close to their fathers and mothers,' said Margherita.

'Children are very little, and fathers and mothers are grown-up,' said the Duchess. 'Besides, there are two parents to every child, and they ought to watch out for him.'

She had a point there, and so I didn't insist. Margherita thought differently, and their argument took an ugly turn, as arguments between women usually do. More than once, the Duchess had said she couldn't stand living with *her* for another minute and had threatened to run away to her grandparents. Now, in the heat of the discussion, harsh words flew from one side to the other, and finally the Red Duchess declared:

'If you would be my daughter, I'd give you a beating with that thing over there!'

At her age, she couldn't have mastered the use of the subjunctive. And the reference to 'that thing over there' was innocent enough, since the object to which she was pointing was a steel mast designed for an Argentine ocean steamer and must have weighed at least fifteen tons. I don't mean to condone my daughter's behaviour, but merely to explain the facts of the situation.

After that, we continued our rounds, but when we came to the women's fashion display, Margherita was so absorbed that the Duchess tugged at my sleeve and said disgustedly:

'The sight of all those clothes makes her silly. Let's us two go on without her.'

I couldn't shuffle off my responsibilities so lightly and so I persuaded her that this was no time to run away together.

'You're just as silly as she is,' said the Duchess, staring at me with utter scorn.

In order to keep out of hot water, I pretended to share Margherita's interest in the latest styles. As a result, when we came to the exit from the fashion salon, we suddenly realized that the Duchess was gone.

After each of us had accused the other of gross negligence, we decided to go halves on the blame. We wandered about like lost souls ourselves, while Margherita punctuated her sobs with word-pictures of tiny bodies mangled by man-eating machines. On the main passageway through the Fair, there was a fountain spouting coloured water into a basin, and Margherita rushed to lean over the edge and exclaim:

'She may have fallen in here and drowned!'

Fortunately at that moment the loudspeaker boomed:

'Attention, please! Will the grandparents of Carlotta call at the Information Desk? Carlotta is waiting there for them. Attention, please, grandparents of Carlotta! . . .'

Margherita came out with a cry of joy. The next moment she looked at me in bewilderment.

'The *grandparents*, they said! We're not the *grandparents*!'

'But she's Carlotta,' I said reassuringly. 'That's the main thing.'

Impulsively we looked around for a taxi, then realizing how idiotic it was to expect to find a taxi in the Fair grounds, we hurried on foot to the Information Desk.

*

The Duchess was sitting in a corner, looking disdainfully at the other lost children, who were bawling like so many branches cut off from the vine.

'Here are your father and mother!' said one of the guards to the Duchess, as he saw us making signs in her direction.

'I want my grandmother and grandfather!' said the Red Duchess resolutely. 'I asked you to call my grandmother and grandfather, didn't I?'

The guard looked perplexed.

'She did say she was with her grandparents,' he muttered to one of his companions, 'and these people are too young for that.'

'We're just her parents, that's all!' said Margherita aggrievedly.

'No, you aren't! That isn't true! I want my grandmother and grandfather!' insisted the Duchess.

The scene that ensued was highly pathetic. We identified ourselves with papers that served absolutely no purpose, because the Red Duchess had no papers to match them and no marks to prove that she was a member of our firm. The guards began to scrutinize us suspiciously and one of them even spoke of calling in the police. At last I had a bright idea.

'Ask the child her grandparents' last name!' I suggested.

Even the most practised criminals have their unguarded moments, and the name supplied by the Red Duchess corresponded with mine.

'Let's go now,' I said triumphantly, and the Duchess came along, bloody but unbowed.

At the door she turned around and pointed a finger at Margherita.

'*She*'s always walking on the grass, where the signs say to keep off!' she said to the guards.

This was quite true. Margherita has a weakness for sitting on the grass of the little park in front of our house, and I've often spoken to her about it. But I said nothing, and for lack of witnesses, the guards let us go.

A Victim of the Silver Screen

WHEN I was a child, we lived only three miles outside the city, but we thought it was at the ends of the earth. The house was isolated and run-down; we had no electricity and water only between seasons, because in summer the well dried up and in winter the pump was frozen.

My mother was a teacher out there for years and hardly ever left home, except when every now and then she revolted and went off on her bicycle 'to live her own life' in the city. As a matter of fact, she did this every Sunday afternoon. She left the house shortly after one o'clock, parked her bicycle somewhere in the outskirts and proceeded by foot to her favourite moving-picture theatre. She went in as soon as the theatre opened and stayed until closing-time, at midnight. Then she called for her bicycle, rode home and came straight to my bedroom, where she said without any introduction:

'It was wonderful! Tragic, of course, but completely absorbing and very significant. He is a doctor, and she ...'

Whenever my mother went to live her own life in the city, I stayed up as late as possible and then read in bed, so that she might find me still awake and plunge straight into her story. Eventually I too went to live my own life, or rather to take a job in the city. But I came home as often as possible, and then my mother told me the story of all the pictures she had seen while I was gone. Eventually I moved to another city, further away, and came home only for Christmas. And my mother had nothing to tell. 'I don't go to the pictures any more,' she said, and I thought sadly that she must be feeling the weight of her years very heavily indeed if she couldn't get on her bicycle and go 'to live her own life' in the city. But that wasn't the trouble.

'I'm bored with going to the pictures,' she explained. 'I don't know whether they've changed or I have. But they don't amuse me.'

I understood the whole thing. My father hated the movies and wouldn't listen to a word about them. So that, in my absence, there was no one with whom my mother could share the story. And that took all the fun out of it.

*

I was working that evening, but at midnight I woke up with a start, to hear a terrific banging of gates, doors and bureau drawers. It's beyond me how every time Margherita comes back from the movies she can make so much noise. Even if I make allowances for the fact that the Duchess and Albertino are with her and do all they can to swell the volume, I still can't understand it.

I was working, as I said before, but at midnight I woke up with a start. There's nothing inconsistent about the fact that I work in my sleep, because my typewriter and the couch in my study are one. I write sitting at the machine, but the ideas for what I write about come to me when I lie on the couch. I sit down to type, but the time comes when I have nothing to say. Then I lie down and think. When I was younger I managed to stay awake while I thought, but now that I tire more easily, I think in my sleep while my body is resting.

On this occasion, then, I woke up to hear one door slam after another, which could only mean that Margherita had come into my study. Indeed, she sat down at the foot of the couch and said:

'It was perfectly wonderful. He was a fellow like you, the sort that enjoys making people suffer. The sort that's unhappy himself and wants everyone else to be unhappy.'

'Margherita,' I interrupted, 'I'm not that sort at all. And what's more, I'm not so unhappy.'

'That's right,' Margherita admitted. 'But if you *were* unhappy, you'd want other people to be unhappy too. Just look at the way you behave when you have a toothache. You're perfectly furious because the rest of us aren't in pain.'

'That's not true,' I protested. 'I'm furious because my teeth hurt and I wish they didn't.'

'That's only human,' said Margherita. 'Everyone wishes he could get rid of his troubles and acquire some of the things he wants in return. Anyhow, if this fellow in the picture reminded me of you, there must be some good reason. The other man in it didn't make me think of you at all.'

'What other man?'

'The engineer. He's as different from you as can be; he doesn't wish his unhappiness on anybody. Although he's wildly in love with her, he shares her happiness when she marries another man, in the belief that she loves him. The truth is that she doesn't love the other man at all, but she thinks that he loves her. And all the time she really loves the engineer, and thinks he doesn't return her love.'

At this point Margherita looked at me out of hostile eyes.

'But the other man doesn't love her,' she went on. 'He has caught on to the fact that she loves the engineer and the engineer loves her, but he pretends that he's in love with her himself, simply so that they can't be happy together. That's what shows him up for what he is. Because when a man's unhappy, it doesn't give him any right to wish his unhappiness on others. If you have to stay up all night to work, you shouldn't envy people that are free to go to bed and try to disturb them.'

Margherita was quivering with indignation.

'Where do I come in?' I protested.

She calmed down and proceeded to the heart of the matter.

'I've just given you the psychological background of the

characters involved. The story is laid in Texas. It begins two years earlier, when he injured his legs in an automobile accident and had to take to a wheelchair. Two years after that, then, when she meets him, he is living just across the street. He writes for a paper (just the way you do) and when she sees him working at his desk (and I forgot to tell you that he's a very handsome young man) they become interested in one another and start talking. Finally, on her birthday, she asks him, along with some of her other friends, to a party. This is the first bit of excitement, because of course he arrives in his wheelchair and she discovers that he is paralysed in both his legs. Of course, that inspires her with pity, and she offers to take him out and push his chair. In fact, it's on one of their trips together that she meets the engineer. She meets him in a railway accident.'

'How come?' I interrupted. 'Does she take him along the tracks?'

'No. Once he has to go to New York to receive a prize for one of his books, and she goes with him. An accident occurs just at the spot where the engineer is directing a job of repairs to the line. The train derails, and although it isn't anything serious, all the passengers have to be transferred to another train across the bridge. The engineer helps effect the transfer, and falls in love with her at first sight. But she is pushing the fellow in the wheelchair and so he imagines that the two of them must be engaged. That's the root of the misunderstanding.'

Margherita went conscientiously ahead with the plot. On account of its subtle psychological character, it didn't seem to promise many surprises, but all of a sudden it grew exciting because of the appearance of Gary Cooper. Gary Cooper was bristling with charm and ready for a fight. After he had got himself into all sorts of complications he suddenly faded out of the story. It seems that he didn't belong in it anyhow, but had appeared in the 'coming attractions'.

When Margherita had freed herself of this interpolation, she worked quickly up to the climax, which was of course the wedding. Since neither of them loved one another, their married life doesn't get off to a very good start and it's obvious that it will end badly. She realized almost immediately that he doesn't love her and married her only in order to make her unhappy. This drives her to hate him bitterly, and here the tragedy begins. One day, when she is taking him out in his wheelchair, they go out into the country and along a deep canal. She goes to gather some flowers, leaving him in his chair, and when she is at some distance she sees something perfectly horrible happen. He has fallen asleep, and the chair is rolling slowly down the bank into the water.

Her first impulse is to shout for help and run to him, but hatred takes the upper hand and she hesitates, without saying a word. The wheelchair goes over the edge and then she is impelled to go to the rescue. He is struggling in the water, but his paralysed legs handicap him and it's clear that he's going to drown. She dives in and swims desperately after him, but her strength gives out and she faints away. Then the miracle happens. When he sees that she is about to die he recovers the use of his legs, swims to her and hauls her out of the water. As the picture ends, they are walking home, soaking wet but happy, because now they love one another.

'I'm glad of one thing, Margherita,' I said with relief. 'You must admit she's really the more despicable of the two. After all, she let the wheelchair roll into the water. She actually wanted her husband to die.'

'The most peaceable woman in the world may be exasperated to the point of committing murder! He remains a warped character, even if he does love her in the end. Because if it weren't for his sudden transformation he'd still be a paralytic and want only to make her unhappy. When you come down to it, he owes her the recovery of his legs. And the engineer is still the better man.'

Margherita brusquely left the room, and a couple of minutes later the Duchess came in and sat down at the foot of my couch.

'What *she* told you is bunk,' she remarked. Then she sighed and went on: 'It was all very silly. He was a poor unlucky fellow in a wheelchair and she was a schemer who married him for the money he made off his book. Then, because she wished she'd married a stupid man who worked on the railway she caused her husband to fall into the water. Afterwards she was sorry and went to get him out, but I have an idea it was all to pull the wool over the eyes of the police. She fainted away and then his legs got well and he saved her. But if I'd been in his shoes, I'd have let her drown.'

'That's not a nice thing to say,' I observed severely. 'It's positively malicious.'

'But she wanted him to die.'

'It shouldn't matter to us what other people do. We must be on the level ourselves. I say he did well to rescue her. And what happened then?'

'They went home together, on foot and arm in arm.'

'In other words, a happy ending.'

'I don't know about that,' said the Duchess. 'I think that she-devil shouldn't have got away with anything short of pneumonia.'

I had to put up a stiff fight to convince her that her hatred of the heroine was deplorable and there was a lot to be said in the woman's favour.

'When a woman wants to kill her husband, I say she's a devil,' the Duchess said categorically.

And, frankly, on this point I couldn't say she was wrong.

'He' and 'She'

HE's dead now, but his restless spirit still wanders about the dark, deserted house. And as it passes before the only occupied room, where I am working, it stops to listen at the door and find out whether *that boy* is really busy or whether he is chatting with *that woman*.

That woman is dead too. She died almost as soon as she came to Milan, as if to avoid giving me trouble, and did it while I was on a trip to Rome, so that when I came back it was all over. I remember that I came by plane and that I looked out at the storm clouds as if I expected to see her spirit emerge from among them.

He waited only long enough for her to be buried in the cemetery of the village where she was born before he followed her there. And it is still hard for me to think of him as my father, having always heard him referred to as *he* and *him*.

'Have you seen *him*?' my mother would say when I came back from the city in the evening.

'Has *he* gone yet?' I used to ask when I got up in the morning.

'Ask *that woman* where she put my things,' my father would grumble.

And when *he* spoke of me to *that woman*, he always called me *that boy*.

In vain do I search my childhood for an image of my father; all that I can find is *him*.

'Don't touch those things. *He* doesn't like it. Don't make a noise or you'll wake *him* up.'

My mother always spoke of him in this manner, and I remember that when I had to call him, I tried in every possible way to get out of saying 'Father'. When there was absolutely no way to avoid it, I remember the unpleasant feeling it gave me.

I always called my mother 'Mother', and it was only with *him* that I referred to her any differently.

'*She* wants to know if you've posted her letter. . . .' 'So-and-so came this morning. I wasn't here, but he explained everything to *her*.'

He is dead now, and no matter how hard I try, I can't think of him as 'Father'. And this saddens me immensely.

*

I was in the dining-room, reading the paper, and all the doors were open. Suddenly I heard Margherita call Albertino.

'Run upstairs and see if he's still in bed.'

I got up and looked into the kitchen.

'I'm up,' I said to Margherita. 'But I'm not *he*.'

'You don't seem to be anybody else,' she retorted. 'You're very much yourself and you got out on the wrong side of the bed.'

'No, Margherita, I didn't get up on the wrong foot. It's something quite different. I don't want you to call me *he* to our children.'

'I never even thought of it,' said Margherita. 'I always refer to you as *Daddy*.'

'Then why did I catch you calling me *he* just a minute ago?'

'I don't know. It just came out inadvertently.'

'That's just the trouble. It came out because you had it inside you. If it hadn't been inside, it would never have come out.'

Margherita leaned out of the back door.

'Children, come here!' she shouted. 'Your father's lecturing on existentialism!'

I said existentialism had nothing to do with it.

'Philosophical nonsense may masquerade under different names, but the substance is always the same,' Margherita insisted. 'And to say that because something comes out means that it's inside comes under the heading of philosophy.'

'Margherita, this is no joking matter, and I wish you wouldn't change the subject.'

'Then don't waste time discussing it with me, Nino. Get busy and bring the question before the Chamber of Deputies.'

I refused to rise to this provocation.

'Margherita,' I said gently, 'it's a matter of egoism, of the healthy kind of egoism that's called instinct. I'll skip the technical aspects, which you know better than I do, and present you with the conclusion that every mother considers her children as belonging more to her than to her husband. A mother's attachment to her child is like the relationship between the earth in which a seed has been sown and the tree that grows out of it. The tree is fastened to the earth by the spreading roots which serve as channels for its nourishment. Actually father and mother have equal rights, but the mother recognizes only her own and is ever ready to defend them. A wife may find it natural enough to divide the possession of a child with her husband, but as a mother she will never cede an inch of it. Even if a wife is on excellent terms with her husband and bound to him by the very deepest affection, the mother within her looks upon the father within him as a natural enemy.'

'And what about the father that lurks within the husband? How does he behave?'

'Margherita, you can't draw up an equation *Mother: Wife* equals *Father: Husband*. There just isn't a "paternal instinct" that can be compared to the "maternal" variety. In an effort to restore the balance, people talk about "the call of the blood", something that no one has ever seen outside a nineteenth-century fairy tale. Right down in the depths of the husband there's practically nobody on guard, because the father is on the upper and outward level. So when maternal instinct carries the attack to the husband's foundations it meets with no resistance and easily knocks out the husband-father team.'

Margherita shook her head.

'Nino, we started on this argument with two characters, and now we're saddled with four. It's all too complicated. Can't you evacuate the stage?'

'It's all quite simple,' I assured her. 'No matter how fond a woman may be of her husband, her maternal instinct is so overpoweringly strong that she can't help quite unconsciously trying to overturn him in her children's eyes. In their presence, she can't resist the temptation to present herself as a martyr, simply in order to draw them more closely to her. It's instinct, Margherita, not *you*. When you're talking deliberately to your children you say: "Go and see if Daddy's awake." But if you're not thinking, then instinct comes to the fore and compels you to say: "Go and see if *he's* awake."'

Still Margherita didn't seem to be convinced.

'Margherita, when you present your husband as *he*, then you're relegating him to the rôle of a stranger, as if he had taken advantage of your weakness to install his mastery in your house. Thus he must be watched so that he won't annoy you, and your children mustn't be afraid to show that they're on your side. In short, when you call me *he*, you gradually exclude me from the family circle; you cut the bonds between my children and me in order to tie them to yourself more closely. In so doing, you weaken the family unit, and damage us, our children, our country and the whole social structure.'

Margherita looked at me hard.

'Giovannino, do you think this thing can be held within our own borders, or is it going to make trouble with the United Nations? Did the fact that I spoke of you as *he* make the relationship between East and West deteriorate still further?'

'Margherita, just keep an eye on that tenant way down

43

in the depths of you! Don't let her get out of control. When you find her explaining to your children that you're *his* victim, that you can't do anything without *his* approval, that if by some good fortune *he's* away overnight, you can all play hen-and-chicks in the double bed while you read fairy stories ... well then, there's the time to clamp down. Send the intruder back where she belongs, by brute force if necessary.'

Margherita shrugged her shoulders.

'I don't like to use force, Giovannino, you know that. And why should I repress the maternal instinct that's been given me for the defence of my children?'

At this point, she stepped back until she was directly in front of Albertino and the Duchess, who were listening in intent silence to what I had to say. Then she threw out her arms, raised her eyes to heaven and said with desperate passion:

'What do you know of mother love? You can take everything away from me. Tear my flesh and step on me! Starve me and send me to die in a ditch; let snow cover my lifeless body! But don't take my children away!'

Automatically, as if they were obeying orders, the Duchess and Albertino stepped forward and stood one on either side of their mother as if to defend her. There were only two of them but together with Margherita they looked like a squadron and there was a look of defiance in their eyes. Margherita stood motionless, a veritable statue of maternal despair, and I got up to leave the room in disgust.

At the doorway I turned dramatically and said, 'Margherita, I beg of you. Don't make a stranger of me in my own home. Don't let the legend on my tombstone read simply: "Here *he* lies." There, at least, let my children read their father's name!'

This appeal to the tomb had quite an effect on the Duchess. She left her mother's side and came over to me.

'Pay no attention!' she whispered. 'She's nuts.'

And we went out to walk in the meadow.

'Is there snow on your grave?' she asked me.

'It's covered with snow.'

'Is it in a very lonely spot?'

'Completely alone.'

'Couldn't you have had it nearer the centre of town?' she asked with a sigh.

I threw out my arms, helplessly.

'Never mind. I'll come to visit it, even in the snow.'

She sighed again and added:

'I'll wear my galoshes, that's all.'

A few minutes later, the other pillar of strength joined us.

'*She* wants to know if you'll look at the water pump. It isn't working.'

So *he* went back and since the water pump was working fine, which *she* knew all the time, they had some tea together.

Sunday

WHEN it rains in Milan, it's not the way it is in other cities, where no matter how noisily it splashes down on to the streets and housetops, you know that it's an extraneous phenomenon and one that you can deal with accordingly. When it rains in Milan – and I'm speaking of the autumn rains – it seems as if the city were a huge sponge, swollen with water, and your most casual step caused it to ooze at every pore. Either it's the effect of the persistent fog, or else it's just that north is north, whatever way you look at it, but anyhow the fact is that instead of saying, 'It's raining in Milan,' it would be more exact to say: 'Milan is raining.' And when the rain ends, the drops that were falling from the sky never reach the ground, but hang for hours in mid-air just over the city.

One morning I walked into Albertino's room and found him at his desk with a notebook open before him. He had pen in hand, but he was staring out of the window.

'Thinking?' I asked him.

'No, waiting,' he answered.

'What for?'

'I'm waiting for it to rain. The teacher told us to write about "A Rainy Day", and I'm waiting for inspiration.'

Very tactfully I remarked that he could write on this subject without first-hand observation. The phenomenon is so frequent that anyone ought to be able to describe it with his eyes closed.

'But it's supposed to be written from experience,' he insisted. 'Experience is what you can touch with your own hand, and anything else is mere imagination.'

Albertino was lucky, for twenty minutes after that it began to rain, and when he was convinced that it was the real thing, he dipped his pen in the ink and wrote: 'It's raining.'

'He's a forthright sort of boy that sinks his teeth right into a subject,' I said to myself, and I left him to his composition.

It rained for over half an hour, and only when the sky was clear did I go back to see Albertino.

'Is it done?' I asked him.

'Yes,' he said.

He had filled five whole pages with: 'It's raining; it's raining; it's raining; it's raining; it's raining; it's raining,' and at the bottom of the last page: 'It's stopped raining.'

'Albertino,' I said gently, 'do you think that's an accurate description?'

'Yes,' he said stubbornly.

'Didn't you notice anything of especial interest?'

'I noticed that it was raining and I wrote: "It's raining." Then I noticed that the rain was over, and I wrote: "It's stopped raining!"'

You can talk all you like about the evils of our day: materialism, existentialism, and the rest. But the real malady is *bare essentialism*. Description of a rainy day: 'It's raining.' Description of your father: 'He's a man 40 years old, 5 feet 9 inches tall, weighing 12 stone and with a moustache.' Description of the first day of school: 'On October 1, I started back to school.' Yes, Albertino is a child of the century.

Not so the Duchess. I enjoy going for a walk with her, because when you add the sophistication of her few years to the ingenuousness of my forty, an interesting conversation is bound to ensue.

Well, it rained that Sunday morning, the way it rains in Milan, and when it was all over and the drops had settled in mid-air, the Duchess and I went for a walk together. We walked until almost noon, and then, just as we were passing in front of a pastry-shop, the Duchess tugged at my sleeve.

'Don't let's forget *her*,' she said. 'If we don't buy *her* something, *she'll* give us the cold shoulder.'

I had to admit that she was right, a thousand times over.

'Yes,' she added with a sigh. 'That's the trouble with having a mother. You have to have her on your mind.'

When we came out of the shop with the box of pastries we saw one of the most commonplace accidents that you can possibly imagine. On the opposite sidewalk, a man stumbled, fell down, hit his neck on the edge of the kerb and lay there, stiff as a board, in the mud, with his eyes wide-open. He had a loaf of bread in his hand, and this was scattered all over the ground. Some passers-by loaded him into a taxi and took him to the hospital, leaving only a pool of blood and some scattered bread behind him. We started towards home.

'He went to buy a loaf of bread and they'll be waiting at home for him to come back with it,' said the Duchess. 'He won't come, and the bread is lying there in a puddle.'

I didn't know what to say, so I tried to change the subject.

'Who is he?' she asked.

'There's no way of telling,' I answered. 'He's just a man that happened to be walking along. Nobody knows his name. This is a big city, and if a man moves from one part of it to another, he's like a total stranger.'

We were walking at a fast clip, but the Duchess was still thinking about the street corner.

'They'll be waiting for him and he won't come,' she repeated.

'He'll be late, that's all,' I told her. 'At the hospital they'll give him some medicine and when he feels strong enough he'll get into a tram and go on home.'

The Duchess didn't say anything, but it was obvious that she didn't believe me. When we reached home, Margherita was setting the table.

'Nino,' she said, 'I forgot to tell you to buy some bread. Do you mind going back for it?'

I started towards the door, but the Duchess barred the way.

'I'm going,' she said firmly. 'I won't fall down, and even if I do, everybody knows me.'

She started resolutely down the stairs, and although she was dragging a bag almost as big as herself behind her, Anita Garibaldi on her horse couldn't have looked any prouder. And I felt protected.

Telephone Service

WHENEVER anyone asks me to do a job or invites me to his house for the evening, I simply can't say no, even if I have neither the strength nor the time to do either. To say no is impolite, and I'd rather be considered a man that doesn't live up to his obligations than an impolite one. For some time Margherita looked down her nose at this way of doing things, and I can't blame her for that, because she had to answer the telephone and account for my failure to turn up where I was expected by saying that I had gone off to Rome, Bologna, Turin, or some other city equally far away.

A lot of people must have come to think that I am a big businessman, with branch offices in the most important cities at home and abroad, because half a dozen times Margherita has said that I was in Zurich, and lately she thought of extending my ramblings as far as France. Well, never mind about that. For some time, Margherita was the victim of my supposed travels, but one day the tables were turned, and when the telephone rang she said to me in great excitement:

'You must answer, Nino! If it's Maria, tell her that I had to go and see my dying aunt.'

This was only the beginning of a widespread epidemic in Margherita's family. I had to answer all telephone calls, including those of my own which I was striving to avoid, and because it was impossible to determine in advance whether a call was for Margherita or myself, I affected a falsetto voice, which couldn't be identified as either my wife's or mine. So it was that many of my friends came to believe that I had a maid.

My telephone duties became increasingly onerous, since I had to answer on behalf of both myself and Margherita. Things took a turn for the better, when early one morning I refused to get up and perform, and Margherita picked up the receiver and said in a bass voice that both her master and mistress were away at Monza. The choice of a place wasn't exactly inspired, but the bass voice was most successful and gave the impression that we had not only a maid but a somewhat stupid butler as well. Everything went on greased wheels, except for the fact that Albertino and the Duchess took an unfortunate interest in the proceedings. When I answer the telephone in a maid's voice, the children have a way of shouting: 'There's Daddy making a fool of himself!' They come and peer up at me, making gestures of obvious scorn and disapproval. Sometimes they even call in their friends to witness my foolishness, and once I caught the grocery boy staring at me with fatuous satisfaction.

*

While I was out yesterday, I called up my wife, and she answered me in a bass voice.

'This is me,' I said.

But so persuasive was the masculine tone of Margherita's voice, that I couldn't help affecting my falsetto, which had the effect of making Margherita persist in her deception.

At this point, I am aware of the weakness of the printed word, for it is unable to convey the different tones of voice of two people engaged in conversation. Since there is no written equivalent to a tone of voice, I must have recourse to some other device. In the dialogue which follows, the words in italics are spoken in a fake voice, and those in roman type are the real thing.

MARGHERITA: *Who's calling?*
NINO: *It's me. Nino.*

MARGHERITA: *Signor Guareschi and his wife are at Lake Como.*

NINO: Come on, Margherita! *It's me, Giovannino!*

MARGHERITA: Oh, is it you, Giovannino? *You?*

NINO: Yes, me ... *No, I mean me, Margherita!*

MARGHERITA: *You* ... No, I'm Margherita!

NINO: *But* it's me, Margherita! *Nino!*

MARGHERITA: *Margherino!*

NINO: Giovannita!

The situation was dramatic. I wiped the perspiration off my forehead and then, making an effort to be calm, put the receiver back to my ear. Across the wires I could hear infernal shouts from Albertino and the Duchess, interrupted by a desperate cry from Margherita:

'Quiet! *Quiet!* I don't know what it's all about, whether I'm *the father*, or *he's* the mother. . . .'

I hung up and sent her a special delivery letter.

*

When I came home that evening, Margherita greeted me with:

'Was it really you that rang up at eleven o'clock this morning?'

'Yes, it was me.'

'Then it was really both of us,' Margherita said with relief. 'I've been worried ever since. These days, life is a continuous adventure, and traps are laid for us within the radius of our own shadow. There are times when one can't help wondering: "Am I myself or am I you?"'

'That's absolutely true,' I admitted.

Margherita stood close to the wall at one side of the window and peered out.

'Our future's as dark as the night outside,' she sighed.

Without saying a word, I opened the slats of the shutters, which happened to be closed, and Margherita regained some of her hope for the future.

The Stranger

IN every family there comes a time when the father wakes up to the fact that there is a stranger in the house. Mothers are different, and since I've never been one of them I had better stick to what I know first-hand.

Anyhow, one fine day I realized that there was a stranger in the house. I remember exactly when it happened. We were sitting around the dinner table and I was passing the family in review. Yes, the usual foursome was present: one Margherita, one Albertino, one Duchess and one Giovannino. Yet I felt that a stranger was among us, sitting right over there, and sure enough, it was Albertino.

Yes, Albertino was the stranger. He hadn't said or done anything new and different, but I had a definite feeling that he was the one. Albertino is only nine years old, but he manages himself very independently. He is reticent and dignified, and in talking to me he limits himself to bare essentials. In the course of a week when he was particularly loquacious, I remember hearing his voice three times. Monday morning he came into my study and said: 'The coffee's boiling over.' Thursday evening, after supper, in the pantry, he raised his head from the book he was carrying round with him to ask: 'What are "antipodes"?' And Saturday, before going away with his mother for the summer, he said: 'Good morning!'

53

Albertino comes to me only in grave emergency. Once, I remember, he told me that his teacher wanted him to bring to class a piece of paper one square yard in size, divided into square feet, with one of the square feet divided into square inches. I must admit that I had to push myself to go to so much trouble. I took a big piece of wrapping paper, drew a square whose sides were each one yard long, then divided it into square feet, and in the upper right-hand foot, staked out 144 square inches.

'Is that all right?' I asked at the end.

Albertino measured the sides of the square yard and then counted the feet and inches in turn.

'One square inch is missing,' he said. 'There are only 143.'

I said that was quite impossible.

'Look here,' I told him. 'Each side of the square foot is divided into twelve equal parts, and since twelve times twelve make 144, the lines parallel to each side can't help forming 144 identical squares. Count them again, and you'll see.'

'Never mind,' said Alberto. 'I trust you.'

This sentence filled me with pride. But I'm getting away from my story. Albertino is that kind of boy, and one evening I woke up to the fact that there was a stranger in the house, and the stranger was Albertino. I didn't say anything to Margherita, because if I had spoken of a stranger in the house, it would have precipitated a whole detective story. Instead, I went and lay down on the couch in my study and waited for something to happen. A few minutes later Albertino came in.

'A boy in my class says you write books,' he told me.

I admitted that this was true.

'I'd like to read them,' said Albertino.

This was something totally unexpected. And my surprise made me feel almost guilty.

'They're right there on the second bookshelf,' I answered, trying to be calm.

Albertino looked at the books on the second shelf one by

one, while I subjected my conscience to a strict examination. No, even in my earliest works, there was nothing unsuited to a nine-year-old child.

'Can I take this one?' he asked me.

It was my latest collection of short stories, and I nodded assent. Later, when I passed by his room, the curtain over the glass door was pulled aside and I could see him reading. When I was alone with Margherita, I confided some of my worries to her.

'He asked to read one of my books.'

'Someone must have told him that you're a writer,' said Margherita. 'That's the trouble with the public schools. The small boys come in contact with the big ones and learn things they shouldn't know.'

When Margherita speaks this way, she isn't trying to be funny. Although she admits that my profession is honourable enough, she thinks it isn't altogether respectable, and every now and then she brings up the damnable question of my university degree.

'Nino, even if you had received your degree and taken a routine job, you could have done your writing on the side. . . .'

Now she simply sighed.

'You shouldn't have given him the book,' she said. 'It was most unwise of you.'

I lost my temper and told her there wasn't a single blush in the whole book.

'But you wrote it, Giovannino,' she insisted. 'Children shouldn't ever read what their fathers have written. If it were a textbook of chemistry, physics or some other science, that would be different. But fiction is to be ruled out, absolutely. Above all fiction like yours, because nobody can be sure when you're serious and when you're joking, when you're sticking to the truth and when you've made up the whole story. There's no telling how he may interpret it.'

'Let him interpret it the way he chooses!' I retorted. 'Lots of people have read my books and found them enjoyable, even people in other countries. I certainly don't intend to flinch before the judgement of a nine-year-old boy.'

Even after I had put out the light, my brain was still working. And that wasn't a good thing.

When I saw Albertino at breakfast the next day, I put on my most nonchalant air. And the same thing at lunch and dinner. The following evening, while I was dozing in my study, Albertino came in. He had my book in his hand, and after he had put it back in place on the second shelf he started to go away.

'Have you finished it already?' I asked him.

'Yes,' he said. 'It's in big print, so it didn't take long.' And he said nothing more.

*

In every family there comes a time when the father wakes up to the fact that there's a stranger in the house. Mothers don't seem to notice. As far as they're concerned, their son is always a baby, with only his mother on his mind. But a father can't be fooled so easily; he knows that the child isn't what he was before. He feels the child's eyes upon him, and they are the cold eyes of a stranger. He knows that he is under scrutiny and that his every gesture will be pitilessly examined. The process is an unconscious one; the boy is studying his father simply in order to find out which one of them is the stronger. The physical side of it doesn't interest him, for he knows that he is on the rise while his father is declining. What he cares about is comparative strength or weakness of quite another kind.

Life is all a cruel struggle, and a man's first enemy is his father. At a certain point a boy begins to study his natural adversary. And because he has instinct for a guide, his judgement is never wrong. Later on, circumstances or reason may cause him to modify his first opinion, but in the final summing-up, instinct will always have the last word. The time comes when a father is made aware that there is a stranger in the house, and the stranger is his son, who suddenly looks at him out of new eyes and takes his measure. The moment is a crucial one, for when it is over, the son has made up his mind. And if he judges his father to be stronger than himself, then he will become his ally.

This is no fun. And yet we must think it out. We cannot be dishonest with ourselves about it.

Heat Wave

IT may be that the heat at the Equator is something like that of Milan. Or, again, it may not run quite so high. I can only tell you what you already know, namely that during this particular summer we all felt as if we were breathing in not fresh air but boiling oil.

'This stinky house is like a furnace,' the Duchess said one day, and Margherita and I exchanged a perplexed look, because we realized that if the heat had seeped down to such a very low level, then it was time to despatch our first battalion.

Our first battalion was composed of the Red Duchess, and we decided to despatch her to the seashore, in the care of an obliging friend of the family. The second battalion, composed of Albertino, did not yet show signs of faltering, and could wait a while longer for relief. Albertino is a man with a personality of his own. When I took him by car to Rome, he read his comics all the way, and when we arrived in front of St Peter's and I announced: 'This is St Peter's, Albertino!' he answered without as much as raising his head: 'I've seen that in my history book, already.'

Now, after the Duchess had remarked that the stinky house was like a furnace, my wife decided to test the reaction of Albertino, who had his nose deep in the Children's Encyclopaedia.

'Don't you think it's frightfully hot, Albertino?' she asked him.

'Couldn't say,' he murmured without taking his eyes off the book.

He was dripping with perspiration, and Margherita pushed the point further.

'Can't you feel the heat?'

'I don't know. When I've finished this, I'll tell you.'

Albertino is not exactly communicative. In the five years that he has been going to school, all I've ever heard is that one day his teacher read a Christmas story of mine to the class.

'What did you think of it?' I asked.

'The teacher reads very well,' was his answer.

Another time, I asked him what the teacher was like.

'I don't know,' he said. 'He's never told us.'

When it came to examination for his passage from the elementary to the upper school, I found out with considerable difficulty that he had to write a composition on 'The Habits of One of Your Parents'.

I asked him which of us he had chosen.

'You,' he answered. 'Mother doesn't have any habits.'

I couldn't help pricking up my ears.

'Well, what did you have to say about me?'

'Nothing too bad,' he said reassuringly.

Albertino doesn't believe in wasting words. He speaks laconically and to the point, and will have no truck with anything but the bare essentials. When someone rings the doorbell and he goes to answer, the message he brings me is simply:

'Man calling,' or 'Woman calling,' as the case may be.

The Red Duchess is anything but thrifty with words and so we decided to pack her off to the shore. Of course, this called for preparations, for you can't send a woman out into the great world, even when she's only six and a half years old, without considerable caution. First there was the choice of a bathing-suit. The green one wouldn't do at all.

'It's too much like the one Mother wore last year. It makes me look old.'

Everything else went smoothly enough, and when she was packed and ready to go she let drop:

'I'm off now. Just ring me up if you need me.'

But in spite of the fact that she could give us her moral support over the telephone, her mind didn't seem to be completely at rest.

'Don't forget to feed the cat,' she said. 'Fruit's not good for him, so be sure to give him meat. And if the cat turns out to be a girl and lays eggs, please let me know.'

We reassured her, but she continued to look around at the dolls and other possessions strewn all over the room.

'My poor things!' she sighed.

Then she recovered her usual aplomb and said to Margherita:

'If *he* wants a cup of coffee or a clean handkerchief, just put it in the basket and *he'll* pull it up with rope. The coffee-cup goes in the special compartment, if you don't want the coffee to spill over.'

Margherita indicated that she got the point.

'When *he's* working, you'll just have to leave *him* alone,' the Red Duchess warned her. 'Husbands are always nervous when they're at work.'

This was too much for Margherita to take.

'You're not going to teach me how to live when you're only six years old! Your business is to play on the beach. I'll take care of your father myself, thank you!'

'If you want to go in my place, I'd just as soon stay at home,' the Duchess retorted.

The argument was growing hot, so I removed the Duchess from the scene and piled her into the car.

'If you really need me, I can come right away,' she told me. 'If *she* bothers you too much, just let me know. Write me on the typewriter. It's easier to read.'

'All right. I promise.'

The car started to move.

'Say good-bye to your wife for me,' the Duchess called out. 'We've had a fight and I don't think we'd better speak to each other.'

And then two enormous, pear-shaped tears came into the corners of her eyes.

'I'm not crying on *her* account,' she protested, and as she saw Margherita coming through the door, her face darkened.

'Good-bye,' she said, looking straight ahead of her and drowning in an ocean of tears. Fortunately at that moment the car pulled away. I know my Duchess. And I know how she suffers when she has to give in to a weakness of any kind.

Meanwhile our second battalion was still deep in his book.

'You might have said good-bye to your sister,' Margherita observed.

'Brothers and sisters don't say good-bye,' said Albertino, without raising his head. 'One may be sorry to see the other go away, but that doesn't call for farewells.'

Margherita sighed.

'What about the Crimea?' she asked a few moments later. 'Does the trouble seem to be spreading any farther?'

'All's quiet in the Crimea!' I told her. 'But if you're talking about the war, then you mean *Korea*.'

'It's all one world!' Margherita retorted. 'Do you think it's going to turn into something bigger?'

'No, I don't,' I told her. 'But my opinion doesn't exactly matter.'

Margherita pressed her head between her hands.

'I can't bear to think of it,' she said. 'I'm still scared to death over the last war. How can I be frightened of one that's not yet begun?'

'It's humanly possible,' I agreed. 'For one woman that's entirely too much. You'd better give up being scared of the war that's gone by.'

Margherita was thoughtful for a moment.

'I think I'd rather give up my fear of the future war, and hang on to the old one. When you exchange an old fear for a new, you don't know what you may be getting.'

This was quite a nugget of wisdom and I was proud of her. Meanwhile, she quieted down and had a chance to notice that the cat was eating an apricot.

'The Duchess said he wasn't to have any fruit,' I reminded her.

'The very idea!' said Margherita peremptorily. 'When for once we have the luck to own a vegetarian cat, we aren't going to force him into being a meat-eater. A cat that abhors bloodshed is a cat that's working in the cause of peace.'

We respected the cat's tastes, and let our thoughts wander towards that first battalion of ours, which was now marching towards the sea.

'It's a funny thing about children,' Margherita sighed. 'When they're here, we're painfully aware of their presence, and when they've gone we're just as painfully aware of the hole they've left behind them.'

We agreed that life is just one pain after another.

'Sad pains and happy pains,' specified Margherita. 'That's why it's no use taking either of them too seriously.'

Bringing Up the Cat

OUR neighbour, Signora Marcella, was at our house on the day of departure, and heard the Duchess' remark:

'If the cat turns out to be a boy, it doesn't matter. But if it turns out to be a girl and lays eggs, please let me know.'

After the Duchess had gone, Signora Marcella gave vent to considerable indignation.

'That child has reached the age of reason. She is a mother of a family!' she exclaimed. 'To think that she can't distinguish a tomcat from a tabby, and imagines that felines lay eggs, like hens or canaries! There are certain essential facts that ought to be made clear even to the very young.'

But Margherita wasn't in the least worried.

'As long as the cat is in the know, that's all that matters. I don't mind if my child is ignorant of certain essential facts, but of course it wouldn't do for the cat to behave like a chicken.'

I found this statement both logical and reassuring, but Signora Marcella didn't agree.

'It's a great mistake to keep children in the dark,' she insisted. 'Even the most old-fashioned educators believe that they ought to be instructed.'

Margherita has a limited number of ideas, but they are all crystal-clear.

'Even the most old-fashioned educators are a filthy-minded lot,' she replied. 'That cat has never had any sexual instruction, but she'll know what to do when the time comes. No one ever talked very much to me about these things, but when I grew up, it never occurred to me to lay eggs like a hen or a canary.'

Signora Marcella isn't the sort to appreciate Margherita's reasoning.

'If you bring a girl up on fairy tales, how can she cope with the crude realities of life when they impinge upon her?'

Margherita was not in the least perturbed.

'How did you cope with them yourself?' she asked. 'After all, you and I were brought up on fairy tales, weren't we?'

Signora Marcella said that times had changed, but Margherita insisted that the famous 'facts of life' were just the same now as twenty years ago.

'I can't think of anything more criminal than taking away the illusions of a child. Fairy tales, as you call them, are like the foundations of a house. You may not see them, but they hold it up through the years.'

This was too much for Signora Marcella.

'What's criminal is to foster those illusions. If a girl's brought up on milk and honey, just think what a shock she'll receive when she learns babies aren't brought by the stork, for instance.'

'It wasn't too much of a shock to me,' said Margherita.

Signora Marcella had a great many things to say, the usual theories put forth by 'sexual planners' the world over.

'I intend to tell my children fairy tales until they're at least twenty years old,' concluded Margherita. 'I still remember the ones that were told to me, and even if I've learned that they aren't true, I continue to get pleasure and comfort from them.'

Signora Marcella insinuated that Margherita wasn't very bright, and Margherita insinuated even more serious things in return, and there the discussion ended. The cat turned out to be a girl, and having attended no courses in eugenics, ignorantly laid a batch of eggs.

I may as well admit that I don't care for cats. In fact, although I treat them civilly, I cordially detest them. Cats may have a right to live, but I'd never allow them to exercise their right in my house if it weren't that my opinion on this score is subordinate to the will of the Duchess. Anyhow, when I say that our cat is a miserable creature, no personal feelings are involved; I am speaking the pure and unadulterated truth. Cats love to display their fertility, but ours was in this respect unusually restrained and brought forth no more than four kittens. For the first three or four days we admired her spirit of self-sacrifice, but because she hadn't taken a course on motherhood, her maternal instinct petered out very rapidly. First she brought the black kitten into the kitchen, where Margherita gave it an enthusiastic welcome.

'Look!' she exclaimed. 'She wants to introduce her children. In just a minute she'll carry it back to the basket.'

Instead of which, she left the pitiful little thing under the kitchen table and disappeared. I restored the kitten to its home, but a few minutes later, the cat deposited the grey one with the white spot at our feet. After I had brought this one back to her, she did the same thing twice over again.

'I think she wants to find out which one, if any, we intend to adopt,' said Margherita. 'She realizes that the task of bringing up all four is too much for her, and since we're such a respectable family, she's willing, for its own good, to give up one of her children.'

I said I wouldn't tolerate her shuffling off her responsibilities in this fashion. She had made her bed and now she must lie in it. Since she had brought these kittens into the world, it was up to her to look after them. But the cat didn't see eye to eye with me, and the next day the whole process was repeated. We found one kitten in the sideboard, one on the bed, one under the store and one on my typewriter. Even after we had restored them to their rightful place and treated the unnatural mother severely, she did not give up hope of foisting them upon us and proceeded to hide them in more recondite places, such as my dressing-gown pocket, one of my shoes, a flower vase and the under side of my pillow. In the final stage of her ingenuity, we could hear the kittens meowing all over the house, but it was impossible to lay hands upon them. Only hunger brought them out of hiding.

Margherita has gone to visit friends in the country, and I am all alone, wondering where the devil that miserable cat will conceal her little time-bombs next. I'm not the kind that drowns kittens. And the Duchess has despatched very definite orders.

'I'm glad to hear there are four babies. Remember to call them Fluffy, Toto, Pecos Bill and Anselmo. But if one of them lays eggs and you know it's a girl, call her Anita Garibaldi.'

There's the Duchess for you! That patriotic touch is what has laid me low. I'm positively inspired by the fact that a minute ago the cat dropped Anita Garibaldi down the back of my shirt. If my country calls, I'll answer: 'Present!' and set out for the wars, doubtless with all four kittens in my knapsack.

Age Forty

MARGHERITA said we must take full advantage of the last days before the children came back from their holidays in the country.

'I intend to have a good time tonight, all on my own,' she declared. 'I'm going out dancing.'

I caught her up on the inexactitude of her expression. You can't very well go dancing without a partner, that is, unless you intend to give a solo performance, and that isn't quite the thing for a wife and mother to do. But Margherita explained that 'all on her own', simply meant without me.

'The main thing is that you shouldn't go along, Giovannino,' she said. 'I'm quite fed up with your face. Night and day, day and night.... It's like the face of Damocles, hanging over me.'

'Have a good time,' I answered. 'I think I'll go to the pictures.'

'Whatever you say,' said Margherita. 'But first you must take me to my night-club. I don't like to be out on the street alone at night. And you can call for me, later on. Of course I could find someone to bring me home easily enough, but I couldn't entirely trust a stranger. You never can tell; he might be a gangster in disguise.'

I took Margherita to the night-club and then pretended to go away. Instead, I sat down at a table hidden by a potted palm, as far as possible from the table where I had left

Margherita. I had only to push aside a branch in order to enjoy a perfect view of the dance floor, her table included. After a while, a talkative young man came and sat down beside me.

'Pretty poor pickings,' he observed. 'All the girls have somebody with them, and a free-lance like myself is out of luck.'

'Don't take it so hard,' I told him. 'I see several women that look as if they were at loose ends to me.'

'Oh, good Lord!' he exclaimed. 'A few overgrown babes that are fair, fat and forty!'

I remarked that a forty-year-old woman may have more to offer than an insipid girl. He admitted the truth of this observation, but maintained it wasn't easy to pick a winner.

'That's perfectly simple,' I told him. 'Just keep your eyes peeled. Remember that it's an acid test for any woman to sit alone in a public place. If she has someone with her, she can always make out; she can giggle, hum, smoke a cigarette, wriggle around in her chair and pretend to be shocked if he tells her a funny story. Or else she can put on a tragic act. She can stare sadly into the distance until the man asks her why she is so unhappy, and that gives her a chance to tell him that she's not like other women because of a secret sorrow in her past. But when a woman's all alone, the way we are, it's a different story. If she can seem to be nonchalant and in perfect command of the situation, then she must have real class.'

My companion looked around at the few lone women in the room.

'There's a dumb Dora, all right!' he whispered into my ear. 'A regular old maid, if ever I saw one! I doubt if she can lift one foot up after another. Straight from the sticks, don't you agree?'

'Do you mean that stout blonde in the green dress?' I asked, pushing aside a branch of the palm.

'No. The one on the left, in the flowered dress, with her handbag on her lap. Can you see her?'

I could see her perfectly. It was Margherita, of course, and she did look as if she had just arrived from the country.

'Look at those legs under the table,' said the young man. 'Mother's little darling must have corns, because she's slipped off one shoe.'

'I don't think she's so bad,' I told him. 'Why not give her a try? Just ask her for one dance, and if that's all you can stand, take her back to her own table and leave her.'

'I'm not in an experimental mood,' he answered.

Finally, after we had discussed three or four other lone geese, he made up his mind.

'I'll try that old gal in yellow there in the corner,' he said grimly. 'If you see that I'm in trouble, call the police. Don't walk out on me.'

My young friend never did come back. I saw him sitting at the table of the woman in the yellow dress, who was gesticulating at him, while he nodded silently in reply, managing every now and then to shoot me a look of utter anguish. It was quarter to twelve, and my poor girl from the sticks was still sitting like a bump on a log, with one shoe off and one shoe on. All of a sudden I sank into one of my sporadic fits of depression.

*

I am in perpetual pursuit of my youth, and this is the source of all my sorrow, because the harder I pursue it, the farther it retreats. There are nights when I follow the street leading to my old school, and peer through the familiar gate, but the wind of time has swept all my words away like so many dead leaves and the darkness is silent as a tomb.

Sometimes I lose my sense of proportion and see the world on a reduced scale, as if through a microscope, with all the infinite fractions between the numbers one and two and the atoms of time between one second and another. Everything around me starts moving; I see my son growing, the apple tree in the garden sprouting, my fingernails lengthening and the paper before me turning yellow. Nothing stands still. All things flow, as the old Greek philosopher had it, and while they evade containment I am overcome by panic and struggle desperately to escape the cursed law of time. 'Stop! Stay the way you are!' I call out to my sleeping daughter and to the chair upon which I am sitting, because I want to halt my youth and look at it again while I still have a chance. But time drags me farther and farther from my past, robbing me of the only wealth I once so fleetingly possessed.

It was quarter to twelve, and my poor girl from the sticks was still sitting alone at her table. I was stricken with panic, because there, behind Margherita, was the elusive ghost of my youth.

*

While everyone else was dancing, I edged my way along the wall to the bar, from which I made a conspicuous entrance to the dance-floor, directly behind Margherita.

'I've come just in time for the last dance,' I said to her. 'Or is it taken?'

Margherita stood up, without speaking, and casually slipped her foot into her shoe.

'A flat tyre, I see,' I said breezily. 'As usual, I suppose you danced every dance.'

'Of course,' she nodded.

'Well, if your feet ache tomorrow, I'll have the last laugh,' I said maliciously.

'We only live once,' she said with a smile.

The last dance was a Strauss waltz, which gave satisfaction to everyone over forty. I whirled about like a Hollywood hussar, and Margherita was as light in my arms as the ghost of my youth.

Country Acres

ONE day when I had completely worked out in my mind the idea of moving the whole tribe to live in the country, I proposed the plan to Margherita.

Her reaction came with the following reply.

'The fact that you have managed to preserve the irresponsibility of your youth is very comforting because it allows you to grow old more slowly than normal men.'

I enumerated all the advantages, both physical and spiritual, that I saw in the move, but this didn't modify Margherita's attitude.

'It's crazy,' she stated categorically.

I dropped the matter then and there. So about a month went by until one fine day at lunch Margherita fixed me with a cold and calculating eye.

This look marks the prelude to our more agitated discussions and while seated comfortably at the luncheon table, I prepared to stand firm.

Margherita attacked with the heavy artillery.

'A stone's throw from here there are open fields, green meadows, the vast sky and fresh air. A stone's throw from here nature unfolds the miracle begun with the creation of the universe. There is the true life close to the soil and *he* won't have it!'

With this she smiled sadly and shaking her head turned to her squadron saying in a tone of resignation:

'My children, let us be patient. We can at least dream of nature, until he denies us even that.'

Victoriously Margherita had swung into a counter-attack, applying her subtle tactic which I call 'the post-humous advantage of the initiative'. The phrase is awkward but the meaning is clear: when I propose something which pleases her, Margherita feels disappointed in the sense that she wishes she had thought of it so that I would have to be grateful to her rather than she to me. So she denies the merits of my proposal.

Then after a certain amount of time has passed, she chooses the right psychological moment to launch, as her own idea, what was originally mine. Her ability is such that she appears on the field of battle, not as the aggressor who tries to impose his ideas on others, but rather as the victim who, lacking the strength of self-defence, bows her head and simply calls the injustice to the attention of public opinion.

Subtly she forces me to accept what I myself had originally proposed. Subtly Margherita takes the posthumous advantage of my initiative inasmuch as the fact that I accept her idea clearly demonstrates to public opinion that the injustice she had opposed was so great that I myself must recognize it and right the wrong.

Thereby Margherita is relieved of any burden of gratitude towards me and in the opinion of the masses I appear as the beaten aggressor while she rises like the conqueror of the oppressor of the people.

If I did not have such great respect for Margherita, I would say that her tactics are typically Communist.

Politics aside, after she had strengthened her position with a deep sigh, she was silent and so was I able to point out,

'Margherita, that is exactly what I want – to get out of the city and live in the country. I have it all planned.'

She sighed again.

'It's too late, Nino. You have recognized your mistake too late. By now the city has poisoned me. It's in my blood. I don't matter. For me it's enough that you frankly recognize your mistake in wanting to live here. Don't move on my account. Do it for your children.'

It was by now perfectly useless to try to regain the initiative.

'All right,' I said. 'We are moving to the country.'

Albertino and the Duchess, having followed the whole affair with intense interest, now felt called upon to comment.

'I don't want to live in the country,' said Albertino.

'I like it here,' said the Duchess.

Margherita rose to the occasion.

'You will do what your father wants. Pleasant or unpleasant, just or unjust, reasonable or unreasonable, a father's orders are followed, not discussed. Just as I have accepted without discussion, so must you.'

Thus it was decided that we move to the country – at least so I thought.

'Margherita,' I said as I sat down at the table, 'do you remember that farm I spoke to you about?'

'No, I don't think I do. Why?'

'Because I've bought it. I made the first payment today.'

Margherita looked at me, wide-eyed with astonishment. Then she turned to the children and said:

'Your father's quite mad.'

Albertino and the Duchess received this statement with total indifference, and Margherita raised her eyes to the ceiling and called upon Heaven to witness my folly.

'He didn't have enough troubles as a newspaperman, I suppose, and so he had to take on a farmer's troubles as well!'

I told her there was nothing to get excited about.

'It's only two and a half acres.'

But instead of calming Margherita, these words had the effect of exciting her all the more.

'For years now, the papers have been talking about acres and acreage, and of course you had to acquire some!'

This is typical of Margherita's logic, and I ought to be used to it by now, but this time I couldn't help losing my temper and telling her not to be silly.

'Silly?' Margherita retorted. 'In all this talk about seizure and expropriation of the land, flood control, and the rest, aren't there always acres involved?'

'Acres have nothing to do with politics,' I objected. 'An acre's just a measure of land.' And I threw the question into Albertino's lap. 'You tell your mother about it.'

'An acre's fifty barrels,' chirped Albertino.

'Don't be a dumb-bell!' I shouted. 'An acre's a square measure, not a liquid one.'

'A decagon,' said the Red Duchess, without raising her eyes from her *Buffalo Bill*.

'What's a decagon got to do with it?' I asked impatiently.

'A decagon's the multiple of a barrel,' said the Red Duchess.

'Stupid!' interrupted Albertino. 'You mean a divisor, not a multiple. And then a decagon's the multiple of a perimeter. Hexagon, heptagon, octagon . . .'

I brought my fist down on the table.

'A hundred and sixty square rods make an acre,' I shouted. 'It can't be anything else but that. And if you'd take your nose out of those comics, and put your mind on your schoolbooks, you'd know that a decagon isn't a square measure at all; it's a plane figure with ten sides and ten angles.'

The Duchess shrugged her shoulders, and Albertino took up where I had left off.

'The decagon's a multiple of the pentagon, which has five sides and five angles. It's a polygon, just like . . .'

I broke in again, but Margherita stopped me.

'Don't take it so hard,' she adjured me. 'It's all your own fault. If you'd bought something in links and chains, the way they used to measure things when I was a girl, there wouldn't have been any of this confusion. Just get this into your head, Giovannino, acres have fallen into the area of political speculation and become elements of disorder. You think you're very clever, but actually you've brought this disorder into the heart of your family. I say these acres of yours are positively subversive.'

After that we called it a day, for I withdrew from the struggle. But in the course of the following evening, Margherita suddenly asked: 'Exactly where is this farm?'

And later she asked what it looked like and whether it was planted with grass and trees. Until finally, one day I heard the Duchess say proudly to a little friend of hers over the telephone:

'No, tomorrow I can't come. We're going to see my father's farm.'

*

After we had rounded the last bend, I slowed the car down.

'Look out,' I warned them. 'In just a minute we'll be at the long side of the lot. It runs all the way to the crossroad, and there it meets the short side, which runs off to the right.'

'What about the other two?' asked Margherita.

'The other two what?'

'The other two sides. Don't tell me they're missing!'

Albertino saved me the bother of making a reply.

'All acres have four sides,' he told her. 'So there must be two more somewhere.'

There I had to put him straight.

'An acre can have only three sides just as well. After all, it's a square measure.'

By this time we had reached the crossroad, and I stopped the car. I backed into the side road and then returned over the stretch we had just covered until we came to the bend where I had alerted the family before. Here I turned round and gave the signal again.

'This time, don't chatter,' I said, 'or we'll muff it again. I'm going to count: "One, two, three . . ." and when I say: "Go!" then you'll know that's the beginning of the long side.'

I started slowly along, counting as I went. When I said: 'Go!' the whole family was overcome with excitement.

'Which one did you say?' asked the Red Duchess.

'Where is it?' chimed in Albertino.

'Did you say on the right or on the left?' said Margherita.

I was furious.

'I told you that the long side runs all the way to the cross-road, didn't I? And that the short side runs from there off to the right. Is it humanly possible for a lot to have its short side to the right of a road and its long side to the left? It's on the right, naturally!'

Meanwhile we had come to the crossroad, and I had to turn round.

'Let's do something with the time it will take us to go back to the bend,' I said to my little crew. 'That way, we'll check our measurements. When I call out: "Stop!" it means that we're at the end of the long side.'

Unfortunately, on our way back to the bend, they had my instructions about looking to the right fresh in their ears. And so, they had been following the wrong side. Now, for the final dash, I once more made everything perfectly clear.

'It might be safer walking,' said Albertino.

'No,' Margherita answered, 'we said we didn't want to make ourselves conspicuous, didn't we?'

I started up the car, and when I said: 'Go!' everyone looked to the right, automatically.

'It's too quick in the car,' Albertino exclaimed when we came to the crossroad. 'Just a second, and it's all over, I want to walk it.'

'Two children wouldn't attract attention,' said Margherita. 'We may as well let them go.'

Albertino and the Duchess started striding along the side of the road, and after a moment of hesitation, I made up my mind to something very rash.

'After all, the place is ours,' I said, 'Why don't we go right in and look it over?'

'What if the farmer sees us?'

This was a rhetorical question, because the farmer had seen us already and was walking in our direction.

'Excuse me,' he said, 'but aren't you the gentleman who's bought the land?'

'Why, yes, in a way I am,' I answered.

'We were just driving by,' put in Margherita, 'and we stopped to let the children stretch their legs. We're moving on right away.'

But he insisted on showing us the farm.

We stopped at the village tavern and had a bite to eat. In the next room, some local people were drinking and talking. A late-comer joined them, and we heard him say:

'It seems the fellow who bought the farm down at the crossroad is here for a visit.'

'What's he look like?' one man asked him.

'I don't know, but he probably looks like a jackass.'

'Of course he does,' said another. 'He paid twice as much for that dump as it's worth, didn't he?'

'Go on!' an old codger put in. 'He's just a poor devil from the city, and they took him in.'

There was a round of laughter.

'I'll bet these new people are going to build a house with a tiled bathroom and a parasol set up in the garden for afternoon tea!'

Margherita looked at me severely.

'Giovannino,' she said, 'is that true?'

'No, Margherita.'

Meanwhile the talk went on.

'You're right. They're going to build a house.'

'And the wife will go around in slacks, as if she were at the beach.'

I looked severely at Margherita.

'Margherita,' I said in a low voice, 'is that true?'

'No, Giovannino.'

The men all laughed again.

'Poor idiots! As soon as they own a few square feet of dirt, they fancy themselves as big landowners and invite carloads of their friends out to see the clover.'

'Well, their house will give us something to laugh about,' said a younger fellow. 'The sort of people that pay through the nose for a piece of land like that are sure to put up a Swiss chalet and imagine it harmonizes with the Po River!'

'Don't I know them? They come out every week to see how the house is going. "Foreman, can you move that door? Do you mind walling up that window and opening another? I want this wall knocked down and a partition put in over there." They like to be told that they're different from everybody else, that they're slightly crazy. Just wait until they get the bill!'

'Well, if he has the money he can spend it as he likes, can't he?' said the old man, who was the most benevolent of the lot.

'You don't imagine he's rich, do you? If he were a real gentleman, he wouldn't build around here. And he wouldn't have bought a mere two and a half acres, either. He's just a would-be, I tell you.'

Margherita shook her head.

'What are you going to do about it?' she asked sadly. 'Resell the land?'

'No, Margherita. As soon as I have the money, I'll put up a house with central heating, a tiled bathroom and a flower garden especially designed for afternoon tea. Every now and then I'll come out to inspect the building, and I'll say: "Foreman, will you move that door a foot and a half to the right?... Will you wall up that window and open another on the opposite side of the room?" Isn't that the proper way for a "would-be" to behave?'

Margherita sighed. When all was said and done, she admitted, the prospect actually pleased her.

'It will be wonderful to get away from the city,' she said, 'and live out here among these simple and understanding people. . . .'

The New House

MARGHERITA insisted that if it was possible to move a wardrobe nine feet high and nine feet wide, then it couldn't be difficult to move a doorway that was only seven by three.

'And don't forget the wardrobe was over two feet deep, while the wall to be pierced is only twenty inches.'

I tried to make her understand the essential difference between a wardrobe and a doorway.

'It's like the difference between a cork and the mouth of a bottle,' I told her. 'It's easy enough to move a cork, but a mouth is a different matter.'

'You'd have to be crazy to imagine moving the mouth of a bottle,' said Margherita. 'But it's even crazier to sleep in the middle of the room just because you can't be bothered moving a doorway.'

This sounds very complicated, almost as if it would take a blueprint to explain. The gist of the problem is this: a room twelve feet square, with the north wall completely free and in the exact middle of each of the other walls, a french window leading to the balcony, an ordinary window and a door giving on to the hall. Since the nine-by-nine wardrobe had to occupy the free north wall, where was the six by six double bed to fit in? All the walls were interrupted, so obviously it had to occupy the middle of the room.

The idea was highly original, and it was healthy too, when you stop to consider all the fresh air that would play around the bed. Only to sleep without being able to lean your head against a wall is as depressingly precarious as to float on a shipwrecked raft in mid-ocean. A self-respecting bed must be firmly anchored to the wall. Or to two walls, in case it's a corner divan. And, in case it fits into an alcove, to as many as three.

An elementary topographical study and a simple geometric drawing revealed another solution. The head of the bed could rest against the hypotenuse of one of the two right-angled isosceles triangles formed by drawing a line from the south side of the door to the east side of the ordinary window and from the west side of the ordinary window to the south side of the french window. This was an original solution, too, but Margherita shook her head.

'No hypotenuse can ever appeal to me as the support for the head of a bed.'

The only answer, then, was to move the door all the way to the north wall and the wardrobe as far as possible to the west. It was at this point that we began to discuss the difficulty of piercing a twenty-inch wall. I walked out on the whole job and left Margherita to oversee it. This was a bad idea, because women love to make one thing symmetrical with another. When I came back later, Margherita was purring with contentment.

'The hardest part is done,' she explained. 'The doorway has been cut through, and only the jambs and architrave are missing.'

I went to survey the scene, while Margherita added:

'I worked it out so that the new doorway is just opposite the one across the hall. A hall punctuated with unevenly spaced doors is extremely ugly.'

Sure enough, the new doorway was splendidly placed, from the point of view of its opposite number. But for symmetry's sake my wife had told the masons to bore through from the hall, and half the doorway opened into an adjacent room. Right in the middle of the aperture was the dividing wall. The masons looked at me in dismay.

'It was the lady's orders,' said their foreman. 'She said she was the boss.'

'Of course,' said Margherita. 'All that's necessary is to move the wall eighteen inches. That will give the bedroom the additional size it needs and cut down the little girl's room, which is too big for her anyhow.'

'No, I won't allow it!' I shouted. 'That wall must contain about half a mile of wires and tubing.'

'Then we'll leave the wall alone,' said Margherita. 'We don't need a door more than eighteen inches wide. The little girl will have an extra door as an emergency exit.'

This wasn't too tragic. Everyone's seen a double-door. The furniture was the only complication.

'It's going to be a bit messy,' I concluded, 'but it can always be brought in from the balcony.'

'Not a bit of it!' Margherita retorted. 'There's a much better system. We can leave the old door open, bring the furniture through and then wall it up.'

This bedroom business was one of the most painful episodes of the new house to me. Not on account of the furniture, which was brought in through the old door, according to plan. The fact is that I had chosen this room for my study and put all sorts of electrical gadgets into the wall: a couple of sockets, a radio attachment (with three openings and a grounded wire), a bell, the plug for an inter-comm phone, one for the telephone and several switches. With a table up against this wall, I should have felt I could give orders to the whole world, that is admitting the world was ready to receive my orders. But as soon as Margherita laid eyes on the room, she picked it out for a bedroom. Now the wall with all the electrical gadgets is covered by the nine-by-nine wardrobe. But when I have to ring the bell or answer the telephone, there is still a way. To bore a hole or two in the thin back wall of a wardrobe is a fairly simple matter, and I know what each hole stands for without hesitation. The bell is behind the second door, just behind my grey jacket; the inter-comm phone is behind the last door, near the pocket of my overcoat, which I never wear.

As for the telephone, it's behind the third door, in a box of moth balls. Of course, this can't go on forever, because the head of the family can't be expected to spend a large part of his time shut up in a wardrobe. But everything works well enough for the time being.

*

To take over a house is a fascinating adventure. The pleasure of tearing down a wall and then rebuilding it in exactly the same place is so subtle as to be positively morbid. A house built for another man inevitably seems irrational to us. We can't imagine why the fellow put a kitchen in the place that was obviously meant for a drawing-room. Or how, year after year, he was able to enter a room through a badly misplaced door.

Another man's house is never adapted to our needs, and I don't see how anyone who has undertaken to build his own house can leave it to an architect to decide where he is to eat, sleep, work and so on. In short, the purchaser's first reaction to the house he has just bought and in which he intends to live is to make it unlivable. He is sorry that he can't take it apart, brick by brick, all the way to the foundations. And to make up for this impossibility, he goes in for superstructures and additions, that is to the extent which the law will allow. For the government regulates the size of buildings and houses in accordance with the width of the street and the fussiness of the employees charged with enforcement of the law.

As we walk about the city, we see new buildings going up every day, buildings in such horrible taste that they take our breath away. These are quite legitimate, but if a plain citizen owns a house and wishes to put in a new chimney or gutter, or make an attic into a store-room, then he has to submit half a ton of plans, tracings, estimates, applications, recommendations, signatures, authorizations and the rest. The fire, police, sanitation and tax departments are all involved, along with the gas and light company, the sewerage plant, the law courts, the bureau of statistics, the automobile club and some twenty or thirty other organizations. Sometimes, the army, navy and air force come in on it too.

But superstructures are a spiritual necessity, and I had to have one. After I had built on an extra room on a symbolical third floor, I even managed to add a tiny bathroom to it. This is the most dramatic part of the story, because both the steam escape and the water pipes of the boiler were close together and both of them were enclosed in asbestos. Well, to cut a long story short, one morning Margherita came out of the cellar in a state of perplexity.

'Giovannino,' she said, 'something seems to be out of order.'

Somehow or other the plumber had connected the bathroom fixtures with the steam escape pipe, and you can imagine the rest.

Moving Day

EVERY now and then we realize that the most common-place things are the most important. Things so common-place that no writer will touch them with a ten-foot pole. Moving day, for instance, is a subject that has been run to death.

And yet moving is a very important matter. First of all, it precipitates an act of self-examination. All your dirty linen is exposed to view, the contents of dark closets and corners under the stairs, of forgotten wardrobes and chests of drawers. Every possession is brought to light, and each one of them brings with it a fragment of the past.

The whole of your miserable existence is spread out on the pavement, and people laugh at it as if it were a show. Failures and sins, large and small, faded pettiness and melancholy and deceit. Old letters and books, outgrown clothes, pencil stubs, a blunted fountain-pen, worn type-writer ribbons, a magazine hidden from the children's eyes, a broken vase with the loose piece that will never be glued into place rattling inside. An army kerosene lamp and a pistol holster thrown down the drain on the last, sad day of the war. Medicine bottles, rusty razor blades, a desk calendar of a year long gone by, an old leather belt and the patented coffee-pot which never would brew.

Here are the crumbs of your misery. Don't throw any of them away, no matter how repulsive it may be, for every collar-button and greasy tie are parts of yourself, something that you have worn until part of you has rubbed off on it, something that you have touched or looked at so often every day that an invisible thread binds you together. You are a creature with all kinds of incrustations. As you stagger through life, every now and then something falls by the way, something that has been a part of your mind and heart.

On the pavement in front of the house you are leaving, there is an exhibition of your pathetic past. Yes, moving day is important, for the act of self-examination which it imposes.

With every passing moment we manufacture a bit of our corpse that is to come. The pile of dead thoughts and accumulated weakness that you had tucked away in dark closets follow you. In your new house you will rediscover all these trivialities of your past. Every now and then you will shut yourself up in the attic and finger the dust, like a thief in the night.

'What's that?' asks your daughter, pointing to one of the heartbeats of your past.

'Nothing.'

'If it's nothing, you may as well throw it away.'

You'll throw it away yourself, one of these days when your father has finished manufacturing his corpse.

The Duchess was wrapping something up, while I looked on.

'That's not a very good job,' I told her. 'It's nothing but a bundle of rags anyhow.'

'It's easy enough to criticize,' she answered calmly, 'but it's not so easy to pack a cat.'

For a moment I didn't grasp the import of what she had said, but my vagueness was soon dispelled, when she set the bundle down on the floor and it began to walk away on four paws.

'Who ever heard of packing a cat?' I exclaimed.

'If you're travelling with a good driver, then it isn't necessary, I agree,' she retorted. 'But with the way you go around the bends, he'd be smashed to bits if he weren't properly protected.'

I promised to take it easy on the bends, and with that she consented to unwrap the cat. In another part of the house, Albertino was stuffing comics into a packing-case.

'I'm not taking them with me,' he said reassuringly. 'I'm just storing them away so the dust won't get at them. They hold a lot of memories for me, you know.'

I noticed that he had taken care of his schoolbooks in a very sloppy fashion, by throwing them pell-mell into a sack, and I couldn't help saying that they'd be better off in the box.

'But I'm taking them along,' Albertino explained, 'and what's more, they don't arouse any memories at all.'

In the dry-goods and clothing department, I found Margherita half-buried under a heap of sheets, blankets and underwear.

'Ever since seven o'clock this morning, I've been trying to divide the necessary things from the unnecessary,' she told me. 'The trouble is that nothing in this world is really indispensable and nothing's superfluous, either.'

I understood the drama of her situation and tried my best to be helpful.

'Margherita,' I said, 'up to a certain period of my existence, I imagined that I couldn't get along without a whole lot of things: a frigidaire, for instance, and my favourite brand of typewriter, hot-water heater, drawing-paper, and desk-lamp. For years, I thought that if I didn't have all my books and a certain kind of "atmosphere" around me, I couldn't write. Then, all of a sudden I found myself deported and in a concentration camp, with nothing but the clothes on my back. Then and there I found out what things were really essential to existence, and with God's help I managed to put them together, and live and think and write just as I had done before. In that wardrobe over there are all the things I had with me during my imprisonment. You can see for yourself that all the essentials fit into one small bag.'

Margherita looked at the bag meditatively.

'Giovannino,' she said, 'if these things are all the essentials, why don't you use them any more?'

'Because I'm not leading the same life as I was then and I don't need to make everything with my own two hands. When I want some hot water, I don't have to heat it over a stove made of two tin cans, and my feet keep dry without my attaching wooden platforms to a pair of down-at-the-heel shoes.'

Margherita shook her head.

'Then, the way things are today, the objects in that bag are no longer necessary.'

'That's true.'

'Then, Nino, why don't you throw them away?'

'It's a matter of sentiment, I suppose. They're so full of memories for me.'

'No, Nino, that isn't it. They're useless, but they're necessary to you all the same. Not to your material life but to your spiritual one.'

I left Margherita immersed in deep thoughts and household linens, and went on to inspect the kitchen, where the maid was in charge of the packing. The maid had no problems of choice; she simply packed everything. She had taken down even the mouthpiece of the house phone from the wall and was just in the process of packing it.

'We won't be taking that with us,' I told her.

'I know. That's what I told the missis, but she said I was to wrap it up just the same.'

I was so curious to know why, that I stuck my nose back into the dry-goods and clothing department.

'Margherita!' I called out. 'There's absolutely no sense in packing the mouthpiece of the house phone. We can't take that along.'

'Take it or leave it, that plastic material is breakable and it won't hurt to wrap it up.'

On top of the radiator in the hall was the regular telephone, wrapped up – after a fashion – by the Duchess. I told her that this too was to be left behind.

'I know that,' she answered, 'but I'm working out here, and every time it rings, it interrupts me. So I decided to shut it up for good.'

Before retiring to my study, I made one more general

tour. Everywhere I found boxes, bundles, trunks and packing-cases. And yet I had said: 'We're taking nothing with us but our personal belongings. Everything else is in the new house already.' But I remembered what Margherita had said, and found I couldn't be angry. Even a broken clock or a leather armchair can constitute a spiritual necessity.

And so, in peace and quiet, I made my own preparations for departure.

Moving a Cat in the Car

HE was the gentlest cat in all the world. I never knew a less catlike cat. He was so little like a cat that to hear him meow was positively startling. Just a short while before the H-hour of our M-for-Moving Day, I saw the Red Duchess holding him. He had let himself be wrapped up like a sack of potatoes, without moving a single claw in self-defence. When we were just about to leave, I picked him up by the nape of his neck and put him into the Duchess' arms. She and her mother and brother were in Carletto's car, while I carried the luggage in ours.

The cat didn't budge, and anyone would have thought he was asleep. But when Carletto started the motor, there was a terrible upheaval and he seemed to have turned into an angry lion. He whistled and howled; as far as I know, he roared and trumpeted as well, and for a moment it seemed as if a whole army of cats were in the car. Finally he slipped through a half-open window and leaped to the ground. A second later he was on top of the tallest tree in the garden. When we had recovered from our astonishment, we called and called and called, but to no avail.

'We'll just have to leave without him,' I decided.

Upon which there was another upheaval in Carletto's car, and in no time the wailing Duchess had slipped out in the cat's pursuit and started to climb the tree.

'If he's not coming, I'm not either,' she shouted.

We all got out of the car and went into the house. Ten minutes later, the Duchess came to join us, with the cat in her arms. This was just about what we had expected, and as soon as the cat was within my reach I took hold of him, put him into a wicker basket and wired down the cover. He didn't resist, and when I looked through the holes in the basket I saw him crouching at the bottom and heard him purr. We piled back into the car, but no sooner had Carletto stepped on the starter than the basket began to dance on the seat and emit a loud noise. Fortunately it was well built and held up against the strain.

We started towards Cremona, with Carletto going ahead, and everything went well until after Pavulo, where Carletto came to a sudden stop. I stopped too, and waited.

'If you ask me,' I said to my friend Al, who was sitting beside me and had the job of stemming the avalanche of luggage in the rear, 'it's going to be the same story all over. First the cat will be out, then the Duchess, Margherita and Albertino in succession.'

Instead, Carletto was the one to leave the car and he came back to speak to me.

'Either put your daughter in a cage, too, or I'm not going any farther,' he threatened. 'The cat is raising a terrible row in the basket, and as a result your daughter is making just as much of a row outside.'

I was disappointed, but my disappointment didn't last long. Out of the window of Carletto's car hurtled a combination cat and basket, the cat having clawed and bitten a hole in the wicker so that now he ran with his front paws free and only the rear paws imprisoned inside. After him came the shrieking Duchess and in a moment they were both out of sight down a dirt track leading into some woods. I asked Al to change to Carletto's car.

'You two go ahead,' I said. 'And I'll take up the slack and follow after.'

Then I drove the car to the beginning of the dirt track and waited. About twenty minutes must have gone by before the Duchess appeared, with the cat in her arms. But as soon as he caught sight of the car, he wriggled loose and ran to look at us from fifty feet away.

'Get in!' I ordered the Duchess. 'Or else I'll sell you for fifty liras to those gipsies encamped up there at the cross-road.'

'I'm not going to leave my cat,' said the Duchess.

'We won't leave him,' I assured her. 'We'll go very slowly, and that way he'll come after us.'

The Duchess climbed into the car and I drove it at a cat's pace for about a hundred yards, after which I stepped on the accelerator and went full speed ahead. If I had had three hands, I might have gone on, but as it was I had to stop after a quarter of a mile, because the Duchess had unleashed a full-fledged people's revolution. As soon as the car came to a stop she slipped out, jumped over the ditch on the side of the road and disappeared behind the hedge. I lit a cigarette and let it hang out of my mouth. That will give you some idea of my nonchalant frame of mind. After all, I could do nothing but wait. I waited twenty minutes, at least, but the Duchess did not return. I got out and called her at the top of my lungs, but the only reply was a gentle meow, and there was the cat, crouching just on the other side of the ditch. I swore at him roundly.

'Where's the child?' I shouted, but I couldn't catch his reply.

Just then a car drew up just behind mine. It was Carletto.

'Didn't you go ahead?' I asked him.

'Yes,' he answered.

'Then why did you arrive from behind me?'

'I don't know,' said Carletto. 'You'd have to ask your wife. Only she isn't here.'

'Where is she?'

'She got out when we met your daughter searching for the cat. The little boy got out too and now they're all three scouring the fields.'

'The cat's here,' I started to tell him, but the cat had disappeared.

We decided that the only reasonable thing to do was to go in opposite directions. Carletto would go back towards Milan and I would continue towards Cremona, and one of us would surely meet them.

'If you haven't found them by the time you reach Milan, then just turn around and come back, and I'll do the same thing when I get as far as Soresina,' I suggested.

Carletto opened the door of his car, but no sooner was he inside than he hurriedly raised the window.

'The cat!' he shouted. 'The cat's on the back seat.'

I helped Carletto to put him out of the car, and then we both drove slowly off. I didn't meet a soul, and at Soresina I turned round and came back. The operation was conducted in an unexpectedly harmonious manner, for Carletto and I arrived simultaneously at the point of departure. The cat was still sitting beside the ditch, waiting imperturbably to see what would happen next. Just then we heard shouts from the direction of Milan and saw our little lost group approaching.

'You might have stopped when I called you!' said Margherita to Carletto. Carletto hadn't seen her at all, and now he tried to explain.

'Never mind,' Margherita interrupted. 'Now the problem is the cat. The little girl will die of a broken heart if we don't find him.'

I pointed him out to her, crouching on the edge of the ditch. He wore an air of supreme boredom and indifference, as if he had nothing at all to do with the tragedy.

Margherita sighed.

'Anyhow, all of us are together. That's the most important thing.'

'Almost all of us,' put in Carletto. 'I don't see Al.'

Indeed, there was nothing remotely resembling Al in the vicinity.

'Didn't he get in with you?' I asked Carletto.

Carletto threw out his arms.

'I don't know a thing,' he stammered. 'All I know is I don't want the cat.'

'Very well,' I answered. 'Reload your passengers, all except for the Duchess, and drive on without stopping until you reach your destination.'

Carletto drove off with Margherita and Albertino towards Cremona, while the Duchess and I remained alone.

'It's not so far, really,' I said to her, 'only about forty miles. I'll go very slowly, and you and the cat can follow.'

I set out, and the Duchess trotted along the ditch for a while, with the cat behind her. Finally she grew tired.

'I'm getting in,' she said. 'Go on just as slowly as you did before, so that the cat can keep up with us.'

I went slowly, and for over a mile the cat followed. Then someone called out to me from a tavern beside the road. It was Al, sitting outside over a glass of red wine, and I told him to get into the car.

'No,' he said; 'I'm waiting for the bus. I have a wife, children and a dog at home.'

I raised the window and started the motor, but a threatening yelp made me take my hand off the gear. The cat was kicking up just beside me, in the Red Duchess's arms.

'Get out!' I said to him, opening the door. But he did not move.

I shut the door and started off. He yelped for a while, but without scratching, until finally he even stopped yelping and the rest of the trip was easy.

When we reached the house the others were not to be seen, and they didn't turn up until three hours later.

'Where have you been?' I asked.

'To Bergamo,' Carletto answered. 'Somewhere I took a left turn instead of a right. But it's just as well, because there we found Al.'

Al was the last to get out. He was shamefully drunk, and, hanging on to a column of the portico, he sobbed:

'I'll never see my home and children again!'

'He's a sentimental sort,' my wife proferred. 'Let him get it out of his system.' And she went on to say that she had actually enjoyed the trip.

We couldn't dislodge the cat from my car. He was fast asleep and we had to take his food out to him in the garage. Eventually he gave up his sit-down strike, but only when he felt sure we were going to stay put. Then he returned to being the gentlest cat in the world, and if anyone stepped on his tail, his meow was as soft as if it came from some other planet.

The Green-eyed Monster

I KNEW very well how things would go, but I had tried to arrange them in such a way as to preserve my sanity.

As soon as we arrived at the new house, we unloaded the luggage from the car and went straight away to the second floor to put the clothes and linen away in the closets and make the beds. For such emergencies, Margherita and I have devised a very efficient system. I work and she directs me. A perfect combination of brain and brawn. And at the end, Margherita invariably has a headache from all the effort I have expended.

Now Margherita promptly took over the direction of our settling-in operation, only this time she had the maid for a supplementary helper on the ground floor, and after spurring me on for half an hour, she left me to my own devices. After a prolonged period of hard work, I heard a sigh behind me, and when I looked around, there was the 'gang' at the door.

'Are we to have rooms to ourselves, or are we to sleep on reclining chairs?' asked Albertino.

'You have rooms of your own,' I answered, dropping my work to go with them down the hall.

'Here!' I said, opening a door to Albertino. 'This is yours.'

'And what about me?' asked the Duchess. 'Where do I sleep?'

I threw open the adjacent door, and said:

'This is for you!'

I went back to my work, and ten minutes later I shouted down the hall for news.

'We're just in the middle of doing something,' shouted back the Duchess.

Just then Albertino appeared in the hall, carrying a bag.

'I found it,' he said to his sister. 'Now we can begin.'

I watched them from a distance, and then, as they became absorbed in their enterprise, I edged up to them. Albertino had unrolled a metal tape-measure and was calculating the length and breadth of his room. After he had written down the figures, he proceeded to measure his sister's room in the same way. I was sure that every detail of the two rooms was exactly alike, including the width of the doors and windows and the colour and quality of the floor tiles and the walls. Meanwhile, the children took a yard-stick to measure the heights of the two ceilings, and these also tallied. Likewise, the doors and windows all faced the same way. The Duchess proceeded to count the units of her radiator, and the distance above the floor of the light switch and the socket in which she was to plug her lamp. So far, so good, but I knew that the most critical point was still ahead. And sure enough, the Duchess announced to me:

'His bed is bigger and better than mine!'

Actually they were the same size and shape and had the same sheets, blankets and mattresses. Only the colour of the bedspreads was different. And in both rooms the chairs were identical. But soon the Duchess found something else to say:

'I have a roll-top desk, but he has a roll-top desk and a bookcase beside it.'

To which Albertino countered:

'There's more room in her desk, because it has three big drawers and four small ones.'

Here I had something to say, because I had planned everything with diabolical care. And so I myself now measured the interiors of every shelf and drawer, under the two children's watchful eyes. After the necessary multiplications, the total cubic contents turned out to be the same.

'There's nothing to argue about,' I said to the Duchess. 'You both have the same amount of storage space.'

'That's what you say,' she grumbled. 'But I don't know how you worked out those sums.'

Just then Margherita came to tell me that one of the young men from the architects' office was downstairs. I sent word for him to wait just a moment, while I closed the windows against a sudden gust of wind and tidied up the work I had left uncompleted. When I went to look for the young man, I found him checking the capacities of the various pieces of furniture in the children's rooms with a slide-rule. Once more, everything came out as it should.

'Aren't you satisfied?' I asked the Duchess.

'I'm not allowed to be anything else,' she said. 'You men are all in cahoots, naturally.'

But I could tell that the equality had been proved to her satisfaction. She dropped out of the picture, and I spoke to the young man about some other things. But twenty minutes later, Margherita came back.

'Your son's crying,' she told me. 'What did you do?'

'I can't imagine,' I said.

When I went with Margherita, there he was, sobbing on his bed. Finally I persuaded him to explain.

'The usual favouritism!' he said between sobs. 'Her light bulb has 75 volts and mine has only 60!'

Margherita shot me a coldly penetrating glance.

'Naturally!' she exclaimed. 'You have no eyes for anyone but your daughter!'

'The truth is,' I retorted, 'that you have no eyes for anyone but your son!'

*

In families with just a boy and a girl, this is the way things always go. The mother suspects the father of being partial to the girl and cruelly unjust to the boy, while the father suspects the mother of prejudice, based on sheer jealousy, against her daughter. Often the children are present at their discussions and continue them on their own hook when they are alone together.

'You're father's pet,' the boy tells his sister.

'And you're the apple of mother's eye,' she answers.

Such suspicion arises between them that they are constantly on guard against one another. And each one considers himself a victim of injustice. This leads to more and more trouble, because fairness demands the attempt to strike an equal balance between them. And here the complication arises from the fact that they don't really need or like the same things. Once I gave Albertino a football, and in order to square things with his sister, I bought her for exactly the same price a magnificent doll. She looked at the two presents and sighed:

'I'm the younger, and so I always get the small end!'

I pointed out the two price-tags and said:

'You don't get anything of the sort. These two cost exactly the same amount of money.'

'I'm not talking about money,' she protested. 'Do you think that an electric motor costing three times as much as a football would be of any use to me? It isn't the price of a gift that counts, it's the utility of it. You can't say a doll's as much fun as a football, now can you? That's why I say I've been cheated.'

'Then what equivalent could I have possibly found,' I asked her indignantly.

'I don't know that,' she replied. 'I'm not my father! If I were my father, then I'd know.'

*

Because I didn't want to have any more trouble of this kind, I had gone to particular pains about the children's rooms in the new house. But all my precautions were foiled when Albertino unscrewed his lamp bulb and found it to be of a lower voltage than his sister's. I woke up to the fact that we couldn't go on drifting. I had to find a radical solution, and one that would benefit the spiritual health of both of them. I must compel them both to bare the sick spot in their souls and then I must perform some radical operation.

'Children,' I announced, showing them a solidly bound notebook, 'I'm so often away from home that I can't follow your psychological development the way I should. It's no laughing matter, because the papers are full of children who have died of some dreadful disease or wound up in prison because their fathers neglected them in this way.'

'Quite right,' said Margherita, whom I had prompted to act as my supporter. 'A little girl died of typhus in Genoa just the other morning.'

'And last month, in Turin, a twelve-year-old boy was discovered to be just as crazy as any adult,' I added.

This last bit of news particularly impressed them.

'What do you mean by *chic*ological development?' asked the Duchess.

'The development of your nervous system,' explained Margherita. 'When someone thinks crooked, then some part of him is physically affected. Like hypnotism, so that you imagine you're cold, even when it's hot outside, and vice versa. Only it's more serious than that.'

Her explanation was quite adequate, and I went on to discuss my idea.

'Every evening before you go to bed, both of you must set down what struck you most of all that happened during the day and what you thought about it. When I come home, I'll read your notes and understand how you've been developing.'

'Do we have to make a rough draft and then a final copy?' asked the Duchess.

'No, one copy will do. You can write with pen or pencil, either one, as long as you make it clear.'

'That's a wonderful idea,' said Margherita. 'A diary with a psychological background. How mysterious and fascinating!'

I went away that same evening, and when I came back, three days later, I was eager to read the children's diaries.

Saturday, 20th
Today my sister and I went bicycling. The river banks and fields were deserted, and we didn't meet a single soul. But I was afraid to ring my bicycle bell for fear of disturbing somebody. I wonder who that somebody could have been.

ALBERTO

99

Today my brother and I went bicycling, but my front tyre was flat.

CARLOTTA

Sunday, 21st
Today a dog went by under my window. He looked up and went right on. Can dogs be in a hurry?

ALBERTO

Today I saw mother reading what Albertino had written in the *chic*ological book. She said he was just as stupid as his father.

CARLOTTA

Monday, 22nd
Nothing happened today. I'm sorry.

ALBERTO

Today I watched the cat.

CARLOTTA

Then there was one last note in an entirely different handwriting:

Children, if I'm still out when your father comes back, tell him that there are cold chicken and cheese in the frig. Children, love your parents.

MOTHER

I found the chicken and the cheese. And as I ate them, I followed the example of the Duchess and watched the cat.

Surprises of a New House

I WENT down to the cellar to try out the furnace. I threw in some paper and wood, and five minutes later the house was full of smoke.

'There's no draught,' said Margherita.

Draught or no draught, if you go up on the roof and drop something down the chimney, according to the laws of gravity, that something ought to reach the bottom. Albertino went up on the roof and dropped pebbles, while I crouched beside the opening in the flue which serves for soot removal, and tried to follow the pebbles' fall. But it was plain that they found no passage.

'You had masons turn the whole house upside down for eight or nine months,' said Margherita, 'and in all that time it never occurred to you to have someone sweep the chimney.'

Everyone knows that a taxi is a vehicle that you find only when you have no use for it, but chimney-sweeps are worse than taxis any day, because you can never find one at all. I removed a few tiles from the roof and stuck a long iron rod into the chimney. After I had poked about for some time, the rod came up against an obstacle of some kind, larger and harder than any mere accumulation of soot.

'When the roof was retiled, probably the workmen dropped a tile down the chimney,' said Margherita. 'Just give it a hard push.'

I hammered at the tile until finally the rod met with no more resistance. But unfortunately, when I tried to push it still farther down, it stuck again.

'The tile is caught a little lower in the flue,' said Margherita.

And with that I resumed my hammering.

Suddenly there were loud cries from the floor below, and we all ran to see what was the matter. The Duchess was crying because she couldn't get out of her room. I couldn't open the door myself, and after pulling at it for a few minutes I asked the prisoner what had happened.

'There's a chain,' she explained from inside.

'I don't remember any chain,' I said, 'but if there is one, try pushing it over first to the right and then to the left.'

'I can't,' said the Duchess. 'There's no handle, and besides the chain runs up and down.'

Margherita was flabbergasted.

'The child must be seeing things,' she said. 'Perhaps she's delirious.'

No matter what the Duchess was 'seeing', it should have given way before a dozen solid heaves from my shoulder. When the door failed to budge an inch, I went outside, took a ladder and climbed in the window.

There was a chain of sorts, after all, made of solid iron and running up and down, just as the Red Duchess had described it, all the way from the architrave to the floor. It was my rod! Yes, masons are very fine fellows when you see them at work in someone else's house, but you see them in a different light when they work on your own. Among the changes I had made on the second floor was the walling up of a certain doorway and the opening of another two yards away. It so happened that in the centre of the new doorway there was a flue, and because the masons didn't want to bother me about such a trifle, they had simply sealed it up in the middle of the architrave. Under such conditions, it is easy to see why there wasn't much of a draught!

Now, the furnace is in working order. But the door of the Duchess' room opens from the inside out instead of from the outside in, and right in the middle of the doorway is a flue

15 inches in diameter, running from the architrave to the floor and carrying the smoke from the furnace. On either side of the flue, a half-door opens, 15 inches wide. Before a heavy meal, all of us manage to squeeze through this space, and no one can say that the Duchess' room is inaccessible.

*

Albertino is a kindly soul, and that is somewhat of a consolation.

One morning Margherita came into my study in a state of great excitement.

'There's something terribly wrong with the electricity,' she said. 'Water is pouring down from the ceiling light in Albertino's room. I turned off the switch near his door and the master switch of the whole house, but the water is still coming. You'd better call up the light company right away!'

Instead of that, I dashed up to the second floor and turned off the tap in the bath-tub. This led to a long discussion with Margherita in which she defended the logic of her supposition by saying that electric dynamos are run by waterfalls and so naturally she had imagined that some pipe at the power-plant was broken. Meanwhile the Duchess had got hold of the vacuum-cleaner and was trying to suck up the big pool of water which had spread from Albertino's room into the hall.

After dinner, Albertino took his mother aside, and they held a long confabulation. They both disappeared, and a few minutes later Margherita came back alone.

'Nino, what are the multiples of a three-dimensional foot?'

'A three-dimensional foot?'

'Yes. I'm helping Albertino with his homework, and we can't figure it out. What's more, we can't seem to establish any relationship between gallons and hours.'

As if it weren't enough for Margherita to have switched off the light in an attempt to stem a flood of water from the bath-tub, now she had to call a cubic foot 'three-dimensional'. I was so disgusted that I called upon Albertino to read me the problem. He began:

'Two taps are pouring wine into a barrel whose capacity is 480,000 cubic feet. How long will it take them to fill it, if the first tap is pouring . . .'

I interrupted him indignantly.

'Who ever heard of a barrel with a capacity of 480,000 cubic feet?'

Albertino threw out his arms in defeat.

The Gate

THE first problem that came with the new house was that of the gate. Now, to open and shut a small, grey-painted iron gate shouldn't give anyone too much trouble. But the matter was complicated by the fact that there was only one key. Whoever didn't have the key had to ring for someone to open from inside. Even if there had been duplicates of the key, we couldn't have given them to the children. Children simply aren't entitled to the keys of the house. And there were still the grown-ups to consider.

At eight o'clock in the morning, Albertino and the Duchess went off to school, and they had to pass through the gate before they could even start on their way. Because there were no servants, either their father or their mother had to get up and open the gate. In this household, the father worked late and never went to bed until four or five o'clock, and the mother was made in such a way that she couldn't possibly assume a vertical position before ten in the morning. So this problem, which wouldn't have existed for a normal family, was one of considerable importance.

I got up early the first day and Margherita the second. The third day, neither of us got up, and the children were vociferously blockaded. That evening Margherita and I examined the question seriously. First, we dismissed the idea of having the children climb over the wall.

'It would be very good exercise,' said Margherita, 'but they might break their necks.'

Then we took up and rejected the idea of making a hole in the wall just large enough for them to crawl through. That would be just the same as leaving the gate open. For disciplinary reasons, we had already set aside the possibility of giving them a duplicate key. Now we thought fleetingly of putting an electric lock on the gate, with a push-button in the front hall. The children would press the button to release the lock, and when they closed the gate behind them it would hold again automatically. But this would require the services of a mason, a locksmith and an electrician and make quite an inroad on the householder's salary. It was at this point that I had an inspiration.

'Margherita, we've looked for an answer too far away. Often the truth is near by, perhaps even within ourselves. It's quite simple really. The children can take the key, open the gate, turn the key twice in the lock behind them and leave it in the letter-box just inside.'

At once we staged a dress rehearsal. Albertino and the Duchess went through the proceedings described above, and I took the letter-box key, opened the letter-box, picked up the key to the gate and opened it also. Then I went out, turned the key twice in the lock and put it back in the letter-box.

'Wonderful!' exclaimed Margherita. 'Now let me have a try!'

In her turn she picked up the key from the letter-box, opened the gate, went out, turned the key twice in the lock and slipped it through the slot for letters. It was nine o'clock in the evening, and we were all gathered outside the gate, shivering from the cold. Margherita and I both had on our dressing gowns and slippers. Just then, she looked at me in perplexity.

'Nino,' she said. 'I can't put my finger on it, but I have a hunch something is wrong.'

'You're quite right,' I told her. 'If we can't persuade the cat to open the letter-box, pick up the key to the gate and let us in, then I think we may have to spend the night outside. And when tomorrow morning comes, we'll still be in the same pickle.'

When we speak of an iron gate, we usually think of a lacework of iron bars, which form a more or less artistic design. And indeed, our gate was of such a kind, except that, on account of the householder's excessive caution, the inner side was backed up with a layer of heavy, close-meshed wire, which prevented any evil-doer from putting an arm through the gate in order to tamper with the letter-box.

Finally we got Albertino to climb over the wall, while an elderly couple walking by made audible comments upon the teachings modern parents gave to their young.

'In my day, a father would have whipped his boy for climbing over a wall,' said the man.

'And mothers don't go out of doors in their dressing-gowns,' chimed in the woman.

Once Albertino was over the wall, everything should have been perfectly easy. All he had to do was open the letter-box, pick up the key and let us in. But ... the letter-box was closed. Margherita had put the key in her pocket. No trouble there however; it only meant slipping it to Albertino. But at this point, Margherita quite unpardonably lost her head and slipped it into the slot of the letter-box instead.

I climbed up the wall, and not without considerable difficulty managed to hoist myself over. But that wasn't all. Margherita came next, and although she had my moral support to help her up and my strong arm to help her down, the operation required a spectacular effort. And no sooner had her foot touched the ground than we heard the plaintive voice of the Duchess from the other side:

'What about me?'

I had to go back over the wall, take the Duchess in my arms, climb up and hand her to Margherita, then fall back and start all over. That made a total of three round trips on my score.

When we reached the house, we lit a fire and warmed ourselves. Then we faced the problem of recovering the two keys. With extraordinary nonchalance Margherita suggested that we unhinge the gate, turn it upside down and shake it. I thought it was simpler to use the same method on the letter-box, and so we did. By midnight everything was in good order. But Margherita sighed:

'I suppose I'm condemned to be a perpetual shut-in. I might as well be buried alive!'

'No, Margherita, this experience was instructive, because it points out the flaw in the system. From now on, the last one of us to go out, must remember to keep the letter-box key on his or her person.'

The next morning the system had its first real trial. At eight o'clock Albertino and the Duchess started off to school. They locked the gate behind them and slipped the key into the letter-box. Unfortunately Albertino put the letter-box key in his pocket, and when I wanted to go out I had to make the climb. The delivery boy threw the groceries over, and at eleven o'clock I came back the same way as before. At noon, when Albertino and the Duchess returned, I recovered the letter-box key and was able to open the gate. But Margherita's nerves were on edge.

'From now on, the key to the letter-box remains in my possession. There'll be no more mix-ups of this kind.'

At three o'clock she went out with the children, and since I was at work in my third-floor study, she locked the gate behind her and left its key in the letter-box, taking the letter-box key with her. At four o'clock someone called me about a business matter, and I had to hurry to the centre of town, climbing over the wall on my way. The children stayed at the house of Signora Marcella, and Margherita came back at six o'clock alone. The gate was locked and the key was in the letter-box which couldn't be opened from the outside. When I came home at eight, Margherita was pacing up and down in front of the gate. Frankly, I didn't feel like scaling the wall again, so we had dinner in a restaurant and spent the night at a hotel.

The next day, which was Sunday, we called for Albertino and the Red Duchess in the late afternoon. I sent Albertino over the wall, slipped him the letter-box key, and he opened the gate.

'This place is a madhouse!' exclaimed the Red Duchess disgustedly. 'I'm sick and tired of it. Some day I'm going to pick myself up and go away.'

'Where will you go?' her mother asked her ironically.

'That's my business!' the Duchess replied.

These days, Albertino and the Duchess are leaving the house through the second-storey window. But it can't go on this way. Either we find some system, or they'll have to stay home from school. Education is all very well, but good health comes first.

Driving Nails into My Coffin

FOR years I dreamed of having a bit of a house of my own and nails to drive into my own walls, real nails, not miserable, brass-headed thumb-tacks. To stick a thumb-tack into a wall is like giving it an inoculation, and inoculations are, to my mind, unnatural abuses of the flesh, like the pierced ear-lobes from which so many women suspend their gewgaws. When I had to learn to shoot a gun, and was forced into a military uniform for the purpose, they stood us in line, naked to the waist, while a big brute of an orderly stuck a hollow needle into every man's chest, near the arm-pit. The needle had a screw top, and as each one of us arrived in front of the doctor, he screwed on a syringe and pumped an anti-typhoid vaccine into us. In this way the government got under our skin and nationalized our recalcitrant bacilli.

As I say, I despise inoculations, and for years I dreamed of having a bit of a house of my own and plenty of nails to drive into the wall; dark, fat nails or shiny nails six inches long. Driving nails into a wall is an incomparable adventure. The plaster is smooth and white, concealing the mysterious irregularities that lie below, and the game consists of finding the point where a nail can be driven in between one brick and another.

When they began to talk about radar in the course of the late, unlamented war, I couldn't take it seriously. I'd like to see radar tell me where to drive a nail into a plastered wall. Because I happen to be a living detector, and if you set me in front of a wall of solid cement, I can pick out on its flawless surface the vulnerable soft spot below.

For years, then, I dreamed of driving nails into a wall of my own. For the nails a man drives into his own walls are the sort of enduring links that transform a house into a home. They are like the act of 'taking possession of the land', which binds the land to its owner forever.

When a man drives a nail into a rented wall, he knows that some day this bond will be broken. When that day comes he may not have the heart to extract the nail, and it remains there like an unused socket, which no longer serves to make an electrical connexion.

At last I got the four walls I had wanted for so long, and needless to say, I held a nail-driving celebration. With every stroke of the hammer I felt that I was creating a new, invisible bond between the new house and myself and striking a new note of music in my vagabond heart. After that, whenever my nerves were on edge and I felt as charged with electricity as a mustachioed storage battery, I knew that these four walls would act as lightning conductors and preserve me from overtension and destruction.

Finally, one day, I realized that the time had come when no more nails could be driven in. Because it would be stupid to think that a man can drive in as many nails as he wants to, even in his own house. Only madmen can ignore man's enslavement to nature's laws. We ordinary mortals know when a place is saturated with nails, just as we know when our stomachs are overloaded. The walls of a house can hold 120 or 572 or 1987 nails, as the case may be, and not one more.

One day, then, I realized that I had driven in the maximum number of nails, and that to drive in even one more would be equivalent to winding the noose around my own neck. I threw away my hammer and looked at all the nails I had driven in. Every one of them gave me as much pleasure as a traveller's backward glance at the road he has left behind him. From this time on, nails interested me only as links between myself and my humble home. No longer did the nails bind me to the house. They became integral parts of the house, and the house bound me to the land, and I felt I should live in this house until the end of my life.

*

'Margherita,' I said one day, 'in which room do you advise me to die?'

She stared at me in perplexity.

'Margherita,' I said, 'when you live in a rented house, you move every so often, or at least there is always a possibility of moving. For many a year we roamed the seven seas, until finally we came ashore, burned our oars and turned the planks of our ship into a chicken-coop.'

'Nino, you're overworking your imagination,' Margherita said severely. 'We haven't a chicken-coop. We have only two miserable pigeons that appear out of nowhere every so often, simply in order to provoke us.'

'Of course, the chicken-coop is strictly metaphorical,' I told her. 'We must have landed among these walls, and among these walls we must die. Just tell me which you think is the most suitable room.'

Margherita put her sewing aside and got up from her chair.

'That's true,' she said earnestly. 'It's someting to think over.'

'Oh, it's not as urgent as all that, Margherita,' I hastened to say. 'God alone knows how many more hours we are to tread the mill.'

'All the more reason why we should give it thought. In this life one has to be ready for everything, including death. Think hard, Giovannino. If you were to be suddenly afflicted with a fatal disease, where would you go to die?'

I shrugged my shoulders.

'The bedroom seems the logical choice,' I replied. 'For one thing, it's roomy. There's plenty of light and air.'

Margherita shook her head sadly.

'And would you find it natural that, after all my grief, I should go on sleeping in your deathbed? That I should brush my head against your pillow and see the last book you were reading on the bedside table?'

This was a reasonable enough remark. I have always been intolerant of egotists, and in my opinion we must die, as well as live, like ladies and gentlemen. Why should I impose such suffering upon Margherita?

'Because the room is so very roomy,' I said, 'we could always put a couch over by the radiator, and I could die there instead of in our bed.'

Margherita sighed.

'It's a shame to go into such morbid details,' she said, 'but now that we've brought up the subject, we may as well see it through. ... You say yourself that the bedroom's the best room in the house, so why should I have to give it up after you're gone? Because the more I think about it, the more keenly I realize that I could never sleep in the room where you had died. It's a matter of delicacy and good taste.'

But the idea of the couch appealed to me, and I couldn't let it go.

'As a matter of fact,' I said, 'the children's room is even more agreeable than ours, and you could perfectly well exchange with them.'

At this moment, the Duchess, who had been listening from the sidelines, actively entered the discussion.

'I won't sleep in the room where you died,' she stated categorically. 'Dead people scare me.'

'The first thing you've got to learn,' I retorted, 'is to respect your father's dead body!'

Margherita shared my indignation.

'Yes, your parents' bodies should be sacred to you,' she said to the children. And then, turning to me, she added: 'Nino, they don't know what they're talking about. But I'm amazed that you should insist upon dying in the bedroom. Wouldn't your study be a much more suitable place? There's a couch in there already, and it's a room where you've spent so much time that you'd feel comfortable and cosy. There's something very heroic, too, about ending your days amid the surroundings where you've worked

113

so hard. It would be like a captain going down with his sinking ship.'

It wasn't a bad idea, and the comparison with a ship's captain was highly flattering.

But at this point Albertino had a word to put in.

'If *she* says she couldn't sleep in a room where you had died, how can anyone expect me to work in one? I'd be the head of the house, you know, and the study would be my headquarters. You always say that the place where a man works ought to be bright and cheerful, and if you die in the study, it will always have sad associations.'

'That's logical enough,' said Margherita. 'The boy has both feet on the ground. Now that I think about it, perhaps the room next to the study is still more intimate and cosy.'

'Nobody's going to die in my play-room!' the Duchess protested. 'I've got my homework to do! And when I'm a little older, my friends will be coming to see me and we'll want to play the gramophone. Surely you wouldn't want me to play dance music in the room where you died!'

'You ought to be ashamed of yourself!' said Margherita. 'Thinking of music and parties already! When I was your age, I didn't think of anything at all.'

'You couldn't have been very bright, then,' said the Duchess. 'But how about the living-room, where you entertain your friends when they come to call? After all, he's *your* husband.'

Margherita branded this suggestion as sabotage, and I didn't like the idea of such a frivolous place, either. We were left with the dining-room and the kitchen, which were excluded. Suddenly I had a new idea.

'The garage!' I exclaimed.

We made an immediate inspection, and decided that, after a thorough clean-up, this would be the perfect place.

'The wide door will facilitate the flow of visitors coming to pay their respects to the body, and also the passage of the coffin.'

Margherita and I sat down on a packing-case to smoke a cigarette.

'Well, we can put that problem behind us,' said Margherita with a sigh. 'The idea of dying in a garage is slightly depressing, Nino, but let God's will be done!'

We were silent for a moment or two, and then I recovered my natural buoyancy.

'What can we know of Fate's designs, Margherita?' I exclaimed. 'Who knows if we shall really draw our last breath in this garage? We may die in a train wreck or an automobile accident, you know. Or perhaps we'll be laid low by a stroke while we're strolling through a flower garden overhanging the sea.'

'A flower garden overhanging the sea!' said Margherita dreamily. 'There's a picture for you! Imagine dying just as the setting sun plunges into the water!'

'I'd rather die at dawn,' I protested, 'when the world is fresh and new. . . .'

After some discussion, we compromised on half-past two in the afternoon, an hour when everything is quiet and motionless under the midday sun. Now, as we came out of the dark garage, we were happy to find ourselves in all the glory of a May morning.

'Life goes on!' said Margherita.

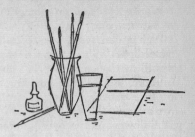

Out of the Frying Pan into the Fire

I ALWAYS speak of my troubles in the past tense, in order to foster the illusion that I have overcome them. Today, for instance, I'm afflicted with every sort of ill, but I prefer to say: At that time I was like an old, broken-down Ford, with a cough in the carburettor, a missing sparking-plug, a knocking heart and an electrical system whose wires had a way of crossing. A hand or foot, my funny-bone, knee-cap, teeth, nose, headlights, or the cartilage of my spine, something was always out of order.

If I kept going, it was thanks to pomades, mouth-washes, bicarbonate of soda, iodine, D.D.T., laxatives, sulfa, mustard-plasters, leeches, phosphates, yogurt, milk and mineral water. One day I called the whole family into session and said:

'It's a serious situation. The motor's held together by an elaborate system of wires and solder. But I can't afford to leave it at the garage for repairs, because it's called upon to work every day. But something's got to be done to bolster it up. From now on this must be the rule of the house: For six days you may all do whatever your consciences allow, but on Mondays Daddy must be able to function with clocklike precision. Daddy has to work Sunday and Monday nights in a row and all day long on Monday, in between, so these daytime hours must be sacred to him. If he is to work with clocklike precision, he must have two things: complete quiet and food that he can digest. For six days of the week, Daddy can afford to have a stomach-ache, but on Mondays he must be pampered.'

Albertino and the Duchess realized that with these words I had no intention of setting up a dictatorship, and they agreed to adapt themselves to the rule. In order to avoid any possible misunderstanding, the Duchess went into the question in detail.

'On Mondays are you free to be angry if the glue has disappeared from your desk or if you can't find either your India ink or your drawing-paper?'

'No,' I answered. 'The disappearance of the glue is not a major infraction. I don't actually use it very often. But every Monday I have to make drawings, and for that reason I can't allow paper and ink to be missing.'

'Very well,' said the Red Duchess, 'that means I'll change my schedule.'

Albertino had only one question to raise.

'On Mondays you are free to be angry if you can't find enough oranges to make a glass of juice?'

'Yes,' I told him. 'The lack of a glass of orange juice might put the whole motor out of order.'

'Very well,' said Albertino. 'On that day I'll make do with apples, pears and whatever other fruit I can lay my hands on.'

Margherita seemed to have no comment to make, but just as I thought they all had the new rule of the house firmly impressed upon their minds, she interposed:

'So I'm a sort of Lucrezia Borgia, that poisons her husband's stomach seven days a week and is kindly requested to lay off for just one day, is that it?'

This wasn't at all what I meant, and I tried to explain it more clearly:

'It simply means that on Monday you must watch out against indigestible dishes. For instance, there shouldn't be anything fried on the menu.'

We were in the kitchen, and of course the Duchess was working with my India ink and brushes on the big table.

'It isn't Monday yet,' she explained when I asked her if I might use them.

'I know,' I answered. 'I only wanted to write up on the wall near the stove: "*No frying on Mondays!*"'

With which I passed from words to action and inscribed this upon the wall.

'It reminds me of certain political scrawls and posters,' said Margherita, shaking her head in a melancholy way. 'Why don't you put: "Our Leader is always right," or: "Believe, Fight, Obey!"'

I protested against this facile sarcasm.

'Look here,' I said. 'By standing up for my stomach on Mondays, I'm safeguarding my output of work and hence the future of our children!'

*

So it was that we came to the first Monday after the Reform. I had worked all the preceding night, and when I got up out of my chair I felt the need of a good glass of orange juice. Sure enough, I found enough oranges in the refrigerator to make a gallon. I went back upstairs and over to my drawing table. My brushes were in perfect order, standing in a yellow jar, and beside them was the bottle of India ink. In the place where I usually kept my glue was a note from the Duchess, which read: 'The glue is on my desk. Don't worry, just go and take it.' I didn't need the glue, so I didn't bother.

The morning went magnificently, and before I knew it, it was one o'clock. Then the house telephone rang and Margherita said it was time for lunch. But even before I heard her voice I got a terrible whiff of cooking oil. Some reader may say that the smell couldn't have come to me over the telephone wire, but must have travelled up the stairs and under the door of my study. But I swear that it was powerful enough to come over the wire. When I walked into the kitchen I had a fit of coughing before I sat down at the table. I didn't say anything, but a few minutes later the Duchess came from school and said, throwing her bag of schoolbooks on to a chair:

'The stink hit me when I turned the corner of the Viale Romagna! Mother, don't you remember the rule about no frying on Mondays?'

Margherita was busily scorching something in the frying-pan, but she turned around to say:

'Mondays? Good Heavens, I thought it was Saturdays? It's amazing the way here in Milan Saturday and Monday resemble one another.'

I didn't want to take advantage of the situation.

'One day is so much like the next,' I said diplomatically, 'that it's quite easy to lose all notion of time. Anyhow, it won't happen again. Every Monday I'll hang a sign on the wall saying: "*Watch out! This is Monday!*"'

And when the next Monday came and I went down to the kitchen early in the morning for my orange juice, I placed the sign near the row of pots and pans hung up on the wall. But when I returned at one o'clock I found Margherita frying.

'Margherita!' I said angrily. 'Didn't you find the sign that reads: "*Watch out! This is Monday!*"'

'Of course I did' she said calmly. 'It was a lovely idea. But while you were at it, you might just as well have added: "Tomorrow is Tuesday!" I didn't see the point of your insistence that Monday is really here.'

Just then the Duchess came back from school and threw her school-bag on the floor, exclaiming:

'Don't you know that on Mondays, in this stupid house, there's to be no frying?'

Then Margherita remembered, but her consternation was so great that I didn't want to make an issue of it. I ate a fried lunch, and the ensuing stomach-ache interfered with my work all afternoon and into the evening.

A week later came the third post-Reform Monday. When I arrived in the kitchen, Margherita wasn't frying, but that was only because she had finished just the moment before, I didn't say anything, but waited for the Duchess, who turned up, as expected, a few minutes later.

'"*No frying on Mondays!*"' she exclaimed disgustedly. 'But on the day between Sunday and Tuesday you always fry!'

And I seized this chance to put in:

'Didn't you see the warning sign?'

Margherita threw out her arms and raised her eyes to heaven.

'Yes,' she said. 'I found the warning that this was Monday and I saw the "no frying" sign too, but I thought that every now and then I might be allowed to break the rule. How am I to plan lunch and supper if I can't fry? I'm just an ordinary housewife without any blue-ribbon cookery courses to my credit. Isn't it only natural that after straining my imagination for so long over dishes that don't require frying, I should give in and smuggle a little bit of calves' brains into the pan?'

It was human enough, I had to admit. I couldn't very well submit her to complete tyranny. Turning to the Duchess I said:

'What about the tube of white lead that belongs on my drawing table?'

'It wasn't in the usual place,' she answered, 'at least not when I was looking for it.'

'I know that,' I told her. 'What I want to know is where it is now.'

'In the kitchen cupboard, next to the tomato sauce,' she explained.

When I had rescued the white lead, I took a brush and painted over the words: '*No frying on Mondays!*'

'You might just as well have left that scrawl,' said Margherita. 'It didn't really bother me. And then it's always pathetic to see an old wall inscription emerge from under a fading coat of whitewash!'

*

At noon on the fourth Monday after the Reform I sat down at the table in an excellent humour. Margherita had concocted an assortment of fried foods, and the smell must have travelled at least a mile away, but my good humour was not upset by that. When the Duchess came in, exclaiming: '*No frying on Mondays!*' I felt even gayer than before.

Margherita brought on the usual bowl of soup, something I adore, but which makes my stomach swell up like a balloon, so that I simply can't touch it on days when I have work to do after lunch.

'No thanks,' I said reluctantly.

'What's the matter?' asked Margherita. 'Aren't you going to have any lunch?'

'Oh, I'm having lunch, all right. But I'm waiting.'

I didn't wait long, for only a little more than five minutes later the doorbell rang and a boy in a white jacket appeared at the front door, with a tray in his hand, from which he proceeded to unload a dish of baked macaroni, one of boiled meat and a vegetable and some stewed fruit for dessert. When he had set all these things down in front of me, he bowed and went away. I started to eat right away, pretending not to notice Margherita's wild-eyed stare.

'This is an insult to the mother of your children!' she finally got out indignantly. 'I've heard of husbands going off to eat in a restaurant, but it really is the limit to have you order a meal sent in.'

The baked macaroni was fluffy and well flavoured, just the way I like it. And when it was finished, I went on with the rest of the meal, paying no attention to Margherita. After I had swallowed the last mouthful I turned to her and said:

'Every Monday I have to work with clocklike precision, not for my own sake, but for the children's, and incidentally for yours as well. If Fate will not allow me any escape from fried food on that day, then I simply must get round it as best I can.'

'It's no use trying to gloss things over,' said Margherita gloomily. 'I count this as an insult of the very lowest degree.'

We remained on these terms when I went upstairs to work. It was a lamentable situation, but my stomach was in perfect working order.

When the fifth Monday came round, I girded myself for battle. But when I came down to the kitchen there was no smell of cooking oil, in fact no smell at all. The table was set, but it looked as if no one had prepared anything like a meal.

Margherita was listening to the radio and Albertino was out in the garden. And when the Duchess came home I could see that she shared my astonishment.

'What do you know about that?' she exclaimed disgustedly. 'Isn't there any more eating in this place at all?'

Margherita didn't answer, and I said to myself that the storm would break when the boy brought my lunch from the restaurant. But it didn't break, after all. The boy brought four servings of everything, set them on the table and went away. We enjoyed the meal in silence, and when we reached dessert, Margherita exclaimed:

'What a relief to have one day a week free from the frying-pan! It's just what I needed. And it's fun to try someone else's cooking.'

No one made any comment either then or during the rest of the week. And so we came to the sixth Monday. At one o'clock I sat down expectantly at the table. The boy came, as before, but this time fried calves' brains were the main dish on the menu.

'Why in heaven's name did you bring something fried?' I asked the waiter.

'This is just what the lady ordered over the telephone,' he answered.

After he had gone, Margherita said:

'After those boiled dinners! They came to be a bore. Every now and then we need a change.'

*

On the seventh Monday, the boy from the restaurant didn't come, for the simple reason that no one had called him. When I came down for lunch the house was full of the smell of cooking oil. And when the Duchess came back from school she wrinkled up her nose.

'If this frying business doesn't stop,' she threatened, 'I'm going to go out for lunch every Monday!'

I took a strong dose of bicarbonate of soda and retired to my study. But there I couldn't find my pencils, brushes or India ink. In their place was a note from the Red Duchess.

'*If all the others are doing as they please, then I'm not keeping up my end of the bargain either.*'

I came to the conclusion that if things were going that way, then there was nothing I could do about it. Perhaps it was all for the best. I put my troubles behind me, and that is why I now write about them in the past tense, although this is the thirteenth Monday after the supposed Reform and at this very moment eddies of black smoke are swirling up from the kitchen, bringing with them the most powerful odour of cooking oil that was ever inflicted upon a human nose. At least I can thank God that the most recent of my many ailments is a heavy cold, which makes this infernal stench seem like no more than an indefinable smell.

Bringing Up Father

EVERY time I come into the pantry, Margherita grumbles: 'So it's you, is it?' And under her breath follow a few well-chosen imprecations. I can't always hear them but I am sure they would provide ample grounds for a libel suit of the first water. As a matter of fact, my entrance into the pantry creates a special situation, parallel to the one created by Margherita's entrance into the kitchen. When the house was remodelled I put a misguided bright idea into execution. This was to cut a large opening in the wall between kitchen and pantry and surmount it with a low arch. Each retained its own character, but the net result was to throw two rooms into one. Now Margherita complains that I'm constantly in her way in the kitchen and I protest against her invasion of the pantry, where I make my downstairs headquarters.

On this particular occasion, Margherita was sitting at the kitchen table and for once she did not grumble. I asked her if there was anything wrong, and finally she spoke.

'We must reach a decision one way or the other. Either *she* leaves this house or I leave it.'

She was working quietly over her scrap-books in one corner, apparently heedless of our existence. I found the dilemma completely unconvincing and simply shrugged my shoulders. But Margherita was in dead earnest.

'Life in this house is utterly impossible,' she explained.

'I simply can't stand it. Pretty soon I'll have lost my self-control altogether. The only thing to do is to solve the problem once and for all. One of us must go.'

The Red Duchess went right on pasting cut-outs into one of her scrap-books.

'What's it all about, Margherita?' I asked. 'Joking aside, I'd like you to explain what *she's* done now.'

'I don't owe anybody explanations!' Margherita shouted. 'It's up to you to decide which one of us is to go away.'

It takes an enormous amount of patience to deal with Margherita. Every now and then she loses all contact with the essentials of the situation.

'Margherita,' I said gently, 'remember that she's only a child, while you are ...'

'Forty-seven!' put in the Red Duchess from her corner.

'Forty-four!' shouted Margherita, shooting a bitter look in her daughter's direction.

'Seven!' retorted the Duchess, without raising her head.

Margherita wanted to jump up, but I held her back and persuaded her to keep her head. What importance could anyone attach to the words of a creature barely three feet tall?

'It *is* important, I tell you,' said Margherita. 'Here at home she does everything she can to set my nerves on edge, and outside she spreads outright slander about me.'

I turned upon the Duchess severely.

'Get it into your head for good and all that both at home and abroad your mother is *forty-four* years old!'

'Very well,' said the Duchess, with her head still hanging low, 'my mother is forty-four years old. But how old is your wife, that's what I'd like to know!'

'Do you see, now?' asked Margherita. 'I tell you she's a snake in the grass! Do you see why I can't stand it a moment longer and why one or the other of us must go?'

Albertino had slipped into the room a few minutes before and was fully informed of the situation.

'All day long she makes trouble for Mother,' he told me.

'She won't do her homework, and she says if they put her back a class, she doesn't even care.'

To hear Albertino side against his sister was most unusual, and I concluded that something must be seriously wrong.

'Is it true that you refuse to do your homework?' I asked the Duchess, advancing with a manifestly hostile air upon her. She was duly warned to give me a respectful answer. There are times when fathers have to be implacable, and this was one of them. Fortunately I know how to live up to my rôle.

'Is it true that you refuse to do your homework?' I repeated.

'Yes,' she answered.

'Take your books into your room and do it immediately.'

'I don't want to go on with school,' said the Duchess, shaking her head. 'I want to work with my hands.'

I told her again to go to her room, and slowly she obeyed. Children know quite well when they are up against a will stronger than their own. Margherita is always shouting at them that they pay no attention. Whereas I raise my voice only when it's strictly necessary, and then they do whatever I say. Now I told Albertino to go and keep an eye on his sister and see that she did exactly what she was supposed to do.

'I make no compromises,' I told him. 'When I give an order, it mustn't be carried out halfway.'

Albertino obeyed promptly, but a few minutes later loud cries came from the Duchess' room.

Albertino came back in a somewhat subdued mood.

'She says I'm a traitor and she doesn't want me for a brother any more.... And I'm not repeating the words she used!'

'Let her alone,' I said decisively. 'She has a personality of her own, and that's something worth cultivating.'

An hour later I decided to look in at the Red Duchess myself. By this time she should have got quite a bit done. To my surprise, I found her with her coat, hat and gloves on, a suitcase in one hand and the cat in the other.

'What about your homework?' I asked.

'I'm going away,' she answered. 'If I stay in this stinky house any longer, I'll end up just as nuts as *she* is.'

Just then Margherita herself appeared upon the scene, thereby complicating things further.

'You'll be happy after I've gone,' the Duchess said to her.

Margherita countered with a number of unimportant remarks, but she made them in such a loud voice that the cat took alarm and jumped out of the Duchess' arm.

'Go on!' the Red Duchess said bitterly. 'Everyone has betrayed me.'

The scene building up in front of me was one of a kind for which I have never had any taste. I evacuated the room and remained face-to-face with the runaway.

'Take off those clothes, put away your suitcase and do your homework,' I told her. 'I'll make no compromise remember, in fact, I'm ready to resort to force of arms! So let's say that I'll be back within an hour.'

When I returned, an hour later, the Red Duchess was sitting at her desk, in front of her notebook.

'Let's see if you've come round to reason,' I said, taking it into my hand.

It was an interesting job, no doubt of that. Obviously she had sat down at her desk, opened her notebook and dipped her pen into the ink bottle. Meanwhile a tear or two had fallen on to the paper. She had placed the point of the pen in one of these tears, and the ink had run down into the tear. Now any artistically gifted person, using a pen, a straw and his or her own fingers to mix ink and tears together, and touching off the result with a drawing pencil, can obtain truly remarkable effects. And if the notebook is closed upon the composition and the wet page comes into direct contact with a dry one, then these effects are highly decorative as well. The Duchess must have shed very passionate tears, because although the notebook was a thick one, the last pages were as sparkling and spontaneous as the first. Only the very last one of all was a variation, centred around a single central blob.

'Did you spit on that one?' I asked her.

She nodded in reply.

'And what about your homework?'

'I'm taking time off, that's all,' she answered.

I said that her behaviour was disgraceful and I should have to give her the punishment she deserved.

'Meanwhile, wash your hands and come down to supper,' I concluded.

I said nothing during the meal, but towards the end, when Margherita brought a basket of apples and oranges to the table, I laid down the law.

'No fruit tonight for a poor student and an unworthy daughter.'

Margherita looked at me in dismay, but I did not relent. I know how to be hard, and I have no fear of being judged unnaturally cruel when reason tells me I should play a strong hand. The Duchess had started to take an orange, but now she opened her hand and drew it back without saying a word. I don't usually eat fruit myself, but upon this occasion I ate two oranges and two apples. After supper we listened for a while to the radio, and then I said that if a certain daughter wanted to bury her head under a sheet and blanket, she was free to do so. With which the Duchess started to leave the room.

'Even the most badly behaved children usually say good night to their parents before they go to bed,' I remarked sarcastically.

'I have no parents,' the Duchess said distantly.

Then she leaned over to stroke the cat.

'So long,' she said sadly.

We sat silently by the radio. Finally Margherita sighed.

'You've never done anything like that before,' she said. 'It was frightful, really.'

'A father that doesn't know how to discipline his children is leading them to ruin,' I replied. 'In a case like this, sentimentality would be a crime.'

'It's not a question of sentimentality,' said Margherita. 'Health comes into it as well. You know that she needs vitamins, and to take away her fruit may be very bad for her.'

I only sneered in reply, and a few minutes later I retired to my study. After several hours, when I was on my way to bed, I decided to see if everything was all right in the Duchess' room. As I opened the door, Margherita's eyes stopped me in my tracks. She and Albertino were sitting side by side on the bed, holding steaming pots and glasses, while the Duchess lay back on her pillow, breathing heavily.

'Murderer!' shouted Margherita. 'You've fixed her properly!'

'She's in a bad way,' said Albertino, looking at me severely.

Even the cat's eyes had a baleful glare. But I wasn't the responsible party. While Margherita and I were discussing the upbringing of children, Albertino had smuggled in to his sister the apples and oranges he had refrained from eating at supper. And after I had gone to my study, Margherita had brought her portion as well. Now the Duchess was bursting with fruit and indigestion.

Of course, my pockets were stuffed with apples and oranges too, but I left them where they were and went to bed. When Margherita came in, half an hour later, she said harshly:

'You simply must stop persecuting your daughter! I don't call that discipline, I call it torture. Tonight you revealed yourself in your true colours and displayed the beast within you!'

Venice, My Watery Grave

VENICE is Venice, everybody knows that; all you have to do is look it up in a guide-book. And Margherita is Margherita, but the guide-books give no clue to just what that means, and so she shall open the story.

A few evenings ago, Margherita was sewing beside the radio in my study, while I lay dozing on the couch. Suddenly Albertino came in with his mother's tape measure in his hand, measured me from head to foot and went away. A few minutes later he came back to measure the breadth of my shoulders. Apparently he had got something mixed up, because he came back a third time, armed with a pencil, checked my shoulders and proceeded to examine my hands and moustache. After that he counted my eyes and ears and jotted the numbers down in a note-book. He seemed bored by the fact that they amounted to two, but slightly more interested to discover that I had one nose, one mouth and three wrinkles on the forehead. All this time I pretended to be sleeping. But I noticed that he counted the number that Margherita and I added up to and wrote down a 2 for that also. Then he stared at Margherita and measured the distance from the top of her chair to the floor. When this was done, he disappeared.

Ten minutes later Margherita left the room and came back with a sheet of paper, which she held out to me without speaking.

Subject of Composition: A Description of Your Parents.

'I have two parents, and my father is five feet eight inches long, lying down, while my mother is four feet four inches, sitting in a chair, with her busy hands working.

'My father has 1 mouth, 2 ears, 2 eyes and 3 wrinkles on the forehead. He has 1 nose and 2 nostrils from which to blow it. Below his nostrils is a moustache 7 inches wide.

'I love my parents, including my father.'

Margherita looked at me wistfully, and being lucky enough to have a nose with two nostrils I proceeded to blow them in order to keep up my dignity. Then I tried to console Margherita by pointing out the touching detail of her 'Busy hands'. But Margherita only shook her head.

'I never knew the measurements of my father when he was lying down or my mother when she was sitting in a chair,' she sighed. 'And if I had to describe my father, I'd never think of the width of his moustache. Our children look at us with the cold eye of a surveyor.'

'Albertino's a very small boy, Margherita. He has plenty of time in which to develop.'

'When he's older and knows more, I suppose he'll write "My father has a net weight of so many stone and my mother a surface of so many square inches." It's the materialism of this new generation in comparison to the spirituality of the old one. When we die, our children will note: "My mother's coffin has a capacity of so many cubic feet," or: "The depth of my father's grave is so many inches."'

Margherita was talking quite loudly, and suddenly the door opened, admitting the Duchess, in a pair of pink pyjamas.

'We can't sleep,' she said darkly.

'Neither can we,' said Margherita, 'although I don't suppose it's for the same reason.'

'I have work to do tomorrow morning,' grumbled the Duchess. 'My green handkerchief needs washing.'

At this point Margherita said that we must defend ourselves, and in fact even counter-attack, and so it was that we decided to take a trip to Venice.

*

Almost as soon as we got to Venice, Margherita bought 36 postcards, but after she had posted 34 of them, she found that her list was exhausted.

'In a case like this, we think too much of other people and too little of ourselves,' she remarked. 'Why shouldn't we send ourselves postcards? You send one to me and I'll send one to you. We'll receive them at home and be happy to see that someone has been thinking about us.'

After we had gone through this little ceremony, we turned our attention to Venice, and on this beautiful day Venice was eminently worthwhile.

'Venice is a city that we all know even if we have never seen it. And no matter how many times we may come here, we can never say exactly what it looks like. In other words, it's a place where we've all been even if we've never actually set foot there, and it seems brand-new even when we come back to it for the hundredth time.'

I said that this might be because we receive so many postcards from Venice and as soon as we get there we spend most of our time sending similar postcards to all our friends.

By now, Margherita had her mind on presents for the children. The Duchess is easy to please, in view of her taste for mechanics, and we bought her a foot-long bolt screwed into the appropriate nut. But for Albertino it wasn't so simple.

'We might get a square and a plumb line,' I suggested, 'so that he can measure us still more accurately for his compositions. And perhaps a thermometer, so that he can record our temperature as well.'

'Don't hold it against him, Nino,' said Margherita with a sigh. 'He's only a victim of this mechanical and uncivilized age, which reduces everything to numbers. "It took us exactly 22 minutes, 15 and 2/5 seconds to get married. The priest was 5 feet 9 inches tall, the temperature was 80 degrees and the ring weighed three-quarters of an ounce." Probably that's how the poor fellow will describe his wedding.'

Here Margherita felt sad over the prospect of Albertino's marriage and said a few hard words about her future daughter-in-law. Then, because we needed a new pot for cooking vegetables, we bought one in aluminium and painted on it in red enamel the words: 'Souvenir of Venice.'

'That's the way to bring up children,' said Margherita, 'to teach them to appreciate the thought that goes into a gift rather than its financial value. It's also a way of combating the materialism of the mechanical and uncivilized age in which we are living.'

It was dark when we got on the boat that was to take us to the railway station, and the lagoon was shimmering with lights.

'Venice!' Margherita sighed. 'We can never leave it completely behind because a part of us lingers on.'

What lingered on was the 'souvenir pot', which we left either at the station or in the boat. And so Albertino's present turned out to be a Milanese fruit-cake which was all we could find in the station at Milan. I wrote 'Souvenir of Venice' across the wrapping-paper and from a sentimental point of view the situation was saved.

The Duchess was thrilled by her bolt. She tied it up in a silk handkerchief and took it to bed along with Giacomo, the carburettor.

'His name is Gigi,' she said, pointing to her new acquisition, 'and he's Giacomo's son. He ran away from home, but now he's come back and everybody's happy.' This story of the 'prodigal bolt' affected me deeply.

Then the Duchess asked me how *she* had behaved and whether she had spent much money.

'Quite a little,' I told her.

Thereupon the Duchess took a parcel from under her pillow, which contained three liras.

'I sold one of my truck wheels,' she exclaimed, as she gave me the money, sighing as if her mother's heedlessness compelled her to stand by her father. And apart from the fact that the truck in question really belonged to Albertino, this touched me even more than the 'prodigal bolt'.

*

A day later I received a postcard from Venice, and for a moment I couldn't imagine who had sent it.

'I'm always thinking of you, no matter where I may be,' said Margherita, and then I remembered the whole story.

'Have you received anything from me?' I asked her.

'Not a thing,' she answered.

When I came home for lunch the next day I found Margherita downcast.

'Still no word from you,' she told me.

'I can't understand it,' I said. 'We posted both cards at the same time.'

'Oh well, it doesn't matter . . .'

Another day went by, and in the evening Margherita was more and more disconsolate.

'Nothing from Venice?' I asked her.

'Nothing at all.'

The next two days, which were Thursday and Friday, I spent away from home. When I came back on Saturday morning I realized at once that Venice had not yet been heard from.

'There's nothing you can do about it,' I said. 'That's the post office for you!'

'That's a man for you!' retorted Margherita.

Monday and Tuesday came next, and on Wednesday morning Margherita said:

'Last night I dreamed you were dead. They fished your body out of the lagoon, and on it was a postcard which you had forgotten to post.'

'There now!' I exclaimed. 'You see that I'm not the kind of "man" of which you are always speaking so badly!'

But Margherita was very upset, and my blood was flowing cold in my veins.

'Giovannino!' she said anxiously. 'Do you think it could be the truth instead of a dream? Mightn't you really be dead there in the lagoon?'

'I was just thinking the same thing,' I told her. 'But here I am, in flesh and blood.'

'Don't you know that there are times when material reality doesn't count as much as imagination? Surely you're not like Albertino, who sums up his parents by their weight and volume. Even if you're here, complete with all your ounces and inches, mightn't I be your widow all the same?'

Margherita is not a reasoning creature and that is why she attains truths that are beyond the reach of reason. After all, reason is a material and mathematical affair. Numbers are bits of matter, or rather, matter is made up of numbers while the higher level of truth is supernatural in character. When Margherita is talking there comes a moment when it's impossible to understand her. I left the house, wondering if I was my own corpse, and didn't come back until late that night.

'Nothing doing,' said Margherita, and I suffered from nightmares all night long.

The next morning we began to scan the papers to see if they carried the bad news. And we bought the afternoon papers as well.

'Perhaps we ought to subscribe to a Venice daily,' Margherita. 'That's the only way to be sure of getting all the local news.'

'I'm pretty well known,' I reassured her. 'If I were to be drowned, all the papers would carry the news, even those of the extreme left wing.'

'That makes me feel better,' said Margherita.

Later, Margherita went to look at the letter-box downstairs, and came back to my study waving something in her hand.

'Here it is!' she panted.

Obviously the card had gone to the wrong address and then followed a roundabout route to the right one. We stared at it for some minutes.

'It's as if you'd come back from Siberia,' sighed Margherita.

'Thank God, that's over,' I said.

'Now we can pick up our lives where we left them,' was Margherita's conclusion.

Just then we heard a tremendous racket in the kitchen. When we reached the scene we found Albertino trying to measure the Duchess.

'I have to write a composition about my sister,' he groaned.

'Neither parents nor sisters are to be weighed and measured, that's what I say!' exclaimed Margherita.

And as a result Albertino's composition was unutterably dull.

'My sister is 1 little girl, with 2 eyes, 2 legs, 2 ears, 2 arms, 1 head, 1 mouth, 1 nose and 2 nostrils, which are to blow.

'I like my sister, but I'd like her more if she were 1 brother.'

The Birthday Cake

THE maid asked if she could go to bed.

'Go right away,' Margherita told her. 'Almost everything's ready.'

'What about the cake and the candles?' the Duchess asked. 'I want it to be pretty for my friends.'

'It will be quite up to specifications,' I told her. 'I'm going to town early tomorrow morning to buy it.'

'You don't have to do that,' said Margherita. 'I'm going to bake a cake.'

It was a serious matter, and the Duchess and Albertino both looked at me in bewilderment.

'Margherita, I don't see any need for your taking so much trouble. You've done too much as it is.'

Margherita shook her head.

'It's a mother's duty to make her children's birthday cakes with her own fair hands,' she insisted.

Her voice had a very decided note, and both children turned pale.

'If you work too hard over it and then get a headache, you'll make me feel very sorry,' said the Duchess.

'I won't complain. A mother must know how to suffer in silence. As soon as we've had our after-dinner coffee, you must go to bed, and I'll start the cake.'

'Are you making an angel cake?' Albertino asked cautiously.

'More likely a double-dyed devil-food cake, if you ask me,' muttered the Duchess darkly, as she got up from the table.

'Be quiet!' shouted her mother.

'It's always the same way,' the Duchess complained. 'When it's my birthday, I always get cheated. You bought a cake for Albertino, didn't you?'

'Well, yours is going to be home-made! And you ought to be ashamed to show so little appreciation of my thoughtfulness.'

'I'm not eating your thoughtfulness; I'm eating the cake!' the Duchess shot over her shoulder.

Albertino followed her, without saying a word, but he gave me an anxious look as he went by. Margherita finished her cigarette and got up from her chair.

'I have a recipe for a very special cake,' she said. 'A cake as soft as cotton-wool and without any of the grease in it that makes most cakes so indigestible. Just eggs, sugar, starch and a pinch of baking soda.'

In order to make the cake really digestible, Margherita should have left out the eggs, sugar, starch and baking soda. But I restrained myself and simply asked her what I could do to help.

'Just light the fire and bring the oven up to the proper heat. But first, measure the sugar and starch. You'll find the amounts on this paper.'

I measured them carefully, then lit a fire in the stove and watched Margherita. She has an unhesitating and decisive way of doing things, and anyone who has never tasted her cakes would say she has a natural gift for baking. It's not that Margherita's cakes are bad. They're simply horrible. This is because she bakes just the way she reasons, pursuing a logic all her own and arriving at the most logically illogical conclusion you can imagine.

Eggs, starch, sugar. Margherita will start off with the idea of following a recipe and beat the sugar and eggs together. But then she can't resist thinning the mixture with a few drops of sherry. At that point, it's too thin, and she adds some grated ladyfingers to thicken it and passes it through a vegetable strainer. She's the Louis Armstrong of the baking world, if you like, only her 'arrangements', unlike Armstrong's music, have to be eaten rather than merely heard.

Margherita worked vigorously for three-quarters of an hour before she handed me a pan filled to the brim with a pale yellow compound and proceeded to give me further instructions.

'Put it in the oven, and check on it every now and then with a toothpick. When you can stick the toothpick in and pull it out again perfectly dry, then it's time to remove it from the oven and let it cool. With a little whipped cream and imagination you can decorate the top; then arrange the candles and put it in the refrigerator.'

She went calmly to bed and I sat down near the oven to keep watch over the cake. Every now and then I opened the door and stuck in a toothpick. The cake remained inert for some time, gradually taking on a golden-brown colour. Then, thanks to the baking soda, it began to rise very rapidly until it touched the top of the oven. After that, it slowly went back to normal, only instead of stopping at the edge of the pan, where it had begun, it sank lower and lower. The toothpick broke when I stuck it in, because a hard outside crust had formed on the outside. I stuck in a nail, which came out sticky, so I closed the oven door again. Just then the Duchess and Albertino appeared in their nightclothes at the door.

'How's it going?' the Duchess asked.

'It's baking,' I answered.

'What does it look like?' asked Albertino.

'I can't say. It hasn't yet taken its definitive shape.'

We waited for ten minutes and then peered in. The cake had sunk lower still, and the nail could hardly penetrate the outer shell. But this time it came out perfectly dry. The cake was done. I took out the pan and set it on the kitchen table.

'It looks like congealed scrambled eggs,' Albertino observed cautiously.

The Duchess tried to pierce it with the nail, but in vain.

'You'll need a cylindrical saw to put in the candles,' she mumbled.

'They can always be stuck on top with rubber cement,' said Albertino.

'I don't think any of that will be necessary,' I told them. 'Once it's been decorated with whipped cream, it will look very handsome, and the candles will go on without any trouble.'

We put the cake in the refrigerator and very soon it was cool. Then we took it out and turned the pan upside-down over the kitchen table. The cake detached itself from the pan and fell with a wooden sound. It looked like a sort of hard, yellow bun, about one inch high, but with a little fingering it stretched to something like its former height, for it possessed considerable elasticity. We stared in silence at what was supposed to be the softest and most digestible birthday cake in the world.

'Poor Mother!' the Duchess said with a sigh, and tears came into her eyes.

'There's no use dramatizing the situation,' I said. 'Let's stage a counter-attack right away. And remember we're fighting not for a mere cake, but for your mother's honour as well!'

I put the cake back in the oven and let it bake until it was dry as a biscuit. Then, forced it through the meat-grinder and mixed the resultant powder with some sweet dessert wine. The result was a most unpromising soupy mixture. I added flour, sugar and eggs, which yielded me a paste, but one which remained gritty even after I had rolled it out on the board, because the powder had brought lumps with it through the grinder.

'We might make a sort of puff-paste and press it with the electric iron,' the Red Duchess suggested.

This gave me a brilliant idea. I cut my present mixture of dough into pieces and put them through the machine for making spaghetti. It emerged from this in flat strips, which I rolled up together into a compact and homogeneous block. But it was very hard, and the Red Duchess observed:

'If we bake it that way, it will be like a brick.'

'And it can't rise, either,' added Albertino.

'Right you are!' I admitted. 'The dough has been un-nerved by the brutal treatment it got in the machine, and we must revive it.'

We dried the block in the oven and then grated it. Then we added more sweet wine, milk and yeast and kneaded it into a comparatively soft substance. After that, we buttered the pan, poured in the new mixture and put it in the oven. When the cake seemed to be baked we took the pan out of the oven and let it cool. Then we removed the cover and used a pair of scissors to trim the dough that had worked its way into the gap between the cover and the pan.

'We should have soldered it with a blow-torch,' the Red Duchess observed.

The cake was cooked, all right, but it was a sad sight, because the top layer had stuck to the cover.

'This is where the iron comes in,' said the Red Duchess, who is a woman that always sticks to her guns.

I elaborated on her idea by sprinkling chestnut flour over the surface to fill in the holes. Then I ran the iron over it and obtained a uniform, shiny crust. On top of this we sprinkled confectioner's sugar. Then we removed the cake from the pan. It wasn't quite as soft as it should have been, but at this point nothing could daunt us. Albertino took the spray from my drawing-table and we watered it with white wine. Whipped cream, nuts, ground sugared almonds and candied fruit went on next as decoration. Three experienced pastrycooks, such as the Duchess, Albertino and myself, could hardly help creating a masterpiece from a decorative point of view. We stuck in the nine candles and consigned the cake to the refrigerator. Dawn was at hand, and weariness weighed down our shoulders. But Margherita's honour had been saved.

*

Towards the end of dinner the cake was brought to the table and scored an enormous success. But when each one of us had a slice on the plate before him, we looked at one another in some perplexity. Who was going to take the first bite?

The brave and generous Duchess was ready to immolate herself and swallowed a big mouthful.

'It's perfectly wonderful!' she exclaimed.

It was indeed a wonderful cake, and Margherita received all sorts of compliments about it.

'Just a routine matter,' she responded indifferently. 'I can do much better.'

The Apple Tree Complex

WHEN I came home for lunch, I was surprised to find the Duchess absent from the table.

'Where is she?' I asked Margherita.

'She's on strike,' Margherita said dryly.

It didn't make sense, and I looked at her in bewilderment.

'She's up in the apple tree,' Albertino explained. 'She stays there all day, and we send her food in a basket. She has a rope with a hook tied on the end to haul it up. The strike's been on since yesterday.'

'What's all this?' I said, turning to my wife. 'Something like this has been going on and you didn't even call me up about it?'

'If I were to call you up every time something out of the way happens, your telephone would be ringing all day long.'

'But what's the matter? What's the strike about?'

Margherita threw out her arms in discouragement.

'The tree's right there, Nino,' she said. 'All you have to do is take a ladder and go and see for yourself.'

I went out and over to the apple tree where the Duchess was perching.

'Stop being so silly and come on down,' I said peremptorily.

Instead of answering, the Duchess climbed up higher. For weeks the newspapers had been full of morbid stories, stories about unbalanced children, who were up to all sorts of crazy things. I went back into the house without pursuing the argument any further. There I found Albertino putting food into a basket.

'No more of that!' I told him. 'If she's hungry, she can come down and eat at the table.'

The meal proceeded, and when we reached our coffee, a glimmer of light suddenly began to dance on the wall opposite the window. Albertino got up, and I asked him where he was going.

'That's the signal she makes with a mirror when she has something to say.'

A few minutes later, Albertino returned with the latest news.

'She says she hasn't had anything to eat since this morning and she's feeling so weak that she doesn't know how much longer she can hang on to the branch. She's afraid she may feel faint and take a tumble.'

Margherita opened her eyes wide, but I motioned to her not to move.

'Go to the garage and take one of those long leather straps off the trunk-holder on the rear of the car. You can send that up to her on the rope and tell her to tie herself to the branch. The safest way is to wind it around her body just below the armpits. That way, if she feels tired this evening, she can go to sleep without fear of a fall.'

Albertino dashed off, and later came back to report.

'She didn't want the strap,' he told us.

Margherita's eyes were as big as saucers, but I stepped right in.

'Albertino, there's a pile of brushwood in the yard. Go with Giacomina and spread a double layer of it all around the tree. That will cushion the shock, and the fall won't be fatal.'

Five minutes later, Albertino and Giacomina came back,

behind them the Duchess, who remained standing at the door. After a minute or two, I asked why she didn't sit down at the table.

'I'm waiting for certain people to go away,' she replied.

'Right you are,' I said. 'There's no worse enjoyment than bad company.'

I went on reading my paper, and ten minutes later the Duchess had sat down and was eating her lunch. I let her alone for a while and then said:

'If you're planning to stay up in the tree, you'd better take some supplies with you. There are cans of milk and meat in the cupboard.'

The Duchess knows how to take it on the chin, and she took this one there squarely. But all of a sudden she began to sob. I turned to Margherita.

'The child isn't well,' I told her. 'We'd better call a doctor. And meanwhile, you may as well take her temperature.'

'Let her alone, Giovannino,' said Margherita. 'Don't forget she's a very sensitive little girl.'

Then Albertino came in.

'It started yesterday morning, when the postman brought her a parcel. She had sent her scrap-book to her old teacher in Milan, and the teacher sent it back with an inscription under the picture of the school. Every one of her old class-mates wrote something on a piece of loose-leaf paper, and when she opened up the scrap-book and saw the picture and all those leaves, she began crying.'

'I don't blame her for being touched,' I said, 'but I don't see why it led to climbing a tree. Where's the connexion?'

'She went on strike,' Albertino explained.

'On strike?' I said in amazement. 'A strike's to protest against injustice. But I don't see anything unjust about a group of schoolgirls sending a token of affection to an old friend.'

The Duchess raised her head.

'The injustice is that their old friend is no longer with them. She's here!'

'This is all beyond me,' I said, throwing out my arms.

'I'm here too, far away from the people I used to work with. But I'm not climbing any trees.'

My ironical tone put the Duchess' nerves on edge and she threw herself sobbing into her big scene.

'He's taken everything away!' she shouted. 'My friends, my teacher, my home! He dragged me out of the city and settled me out here in a hovel!... I had all I wanted before, and now I have nothing!... Here you have to ride a bicycle for miles to find so much as a newspaper.... And if you want to see anybody, well, you can feast your eyes on cows and chickens.... As for pictures, there are only those antiques they show in the parish house.... There's no use wearing good clothes, because there's always six inches of dust or mud outside!... If you want to roller-skate, you can't go on the pavement, because the pavement's made of stepping-stones, and even when you're walking you may fall and break your neck!... He's taken away everything ... everything, I tell you! And then he has the nerve to say he doesn't know why I feel like climbing a tree!... What does he care?'

And the big scene dissolved in an ocean of tears.

I counter-attacked without delay.

'I still don't understand,' I insisted. 'All these things that have been taken away from you have been taken away from your brother as well. But he doesn't seem to be sorry.'

'What of it?' the Duchess retorted. 'He's a man. As long as he has all he wants to eat and drink, he'd just as soon be here as in Milan.'

'Your brother isn't limited to eating and drinking,' I put in. 'His spiritual needs are greater than yours, if you want to know, but he seems to find plenty of satisfaction. And don't forget the country's good for your health. You look much better than you ever did in town.'

'I don't care about my health!' the Duchess retorted. 'What's it matter how well I look outside, if inside I have a *pomplex*?'

'A complex, you mean.'

'All right, a complex. What your wife gets, when she feels as if she were shipwrecked on a desert island, all alone.'

'This is no desert island,' I said, shaking my head. 'This is a quiet country village, an oasis of peace, a front seat at the greatest of all shows, put on by nature. Violets on the river banks, green trees, and fresh, clean air? What do you say to all those? And the breath of the open sky? The songs of the birds? The repose of it all? You can't have any of these things in the city.'

But the Duchess did not give up.

'You can't have them, that's true. But every time you think about them, you say: "How wonderful!" And out here, where they're all around, no one pays any attention, and so they don't matter.'

I decided it was time to settle things once and for all.

'I gather from all this,' I said to the Duchess, 'that your life here is unbearable and you suffer intensely. Now I'd like to hear what your mother has to say.'

Margherita was smoking and turning over the pages of a picture magazine.

'Are you talking to me?' she asked.

'Yes. I'd like to know what you think of this life we're leading. Does it suit you, or are you suffering, like your daughter?'

'I can't possibly have any opinion,' Margherita answered. 'I'm just a member of your little crew. Wherever the ship takes me, I must go. You're at the helm. And the sufferings of the crew don't count. *Navigare necesse est*, as Columbus used to say. We must sail on and on and on.'

'Very well,' I said. 'I get it. Tomorrow you must leave the ship and go back to Milan, while I stay here. It won't make much difference in the long run. I'll live just as long here as I would in the city.'

*

That evening, after supper, I inquired about the intentions of the crew.

'Are you off tomorrow?' I asked.

Margherita shot me a cold look.

'Off where?'

'Off to Milan.'

'Don't be silly,' she said, stiffening. 'I'm quite all right here, and here I'm going to stay. I'd rather suffer in silence here than in Milan!'

'Me too,' said the Duchess.

I turned to Albertino.

'What about you?'

'I'm not suffering,' he answered calmly.

'Us women are the ones to suffer,' said the Duchess.

I thought that sally might very well close the scene. So I figuratively pulled down the curtain and explained the moral of it all to Albertino.

'My boy, men and women are both born to suffer. But women are especially born to tell their husbands about it. A woman suffers most when everything is going well, because then it's difficult, in fact almost impossible, to make her suffering seem real. My boy, if you don't want to make your wife suffer, here's what you must do. You must not only look after her well-being, but you must also tell her that you realize she is suffering in silence for you.'

Albertino gave me a puzzled look.

'It's all very complicated,' he said.

'Not a bit of it! You only have to remember that within every woman, even the happiest, there is a suffering double.'

'And do you have to marry them both?' asked Albertino.

'Naturally, my boy. There's no getting away from it. That's the big mistake in saying: "It takes two to get married." Because it takes three, two women and one man. One of the women says "Yes" to you in an outburst of joy, while the other chimes in with silent sorrow.'

Family Tree

I THOUGHT we had settled the tree question until Margherita came into the room all of a sudden with an unaccustomed glimmer in her eyes.

'It's all over!' she stated almost aggressively. 'Until yesterday I was up against your overwhelming personality, defenceless and alone. But now I have a Pope and a long line of Counts behind me.'

All I could see behind her was a large wardrobe, and this didn't particularly impress me. Margherita perceived my indifference and proceeded further.

'Every one of us has the glorious past of his ancestors behind him. His temporal body is, if you like, the sheath of the present, which envelops this past. When a man dies he loses the present and becomes the past of his descendants. Today you are simply what you are, but tomorrow you will be transformed into an ancestor.'

I said that this was all very well, but that I failed to see where a Pope and Counts came into it.

'It's quite simple, really,' said Margherita. 'It has just been discovered, entirely by accident, that among my ancestors are a Pope and a long line of Counts.'

'"*Accounts*" did you say?' asked the Duchess, as she pushed open the door of my study with a pile of letters for me in her hand. 'Unpaid accounts, I take it.'

Margherita looked at her disgustedly.

'Your mind runs along the same lines as your father's,' she observed.

'And who can my father be?' the Duchess asked me.

'I think he's the man that comes to read the gas meter,' I told her.

'Just what I thought,' said the Red Duchess indifferently as she went out of the room.

'If she were a man, I'd slap her for that,' said Margherita; 'and if you were a woman, I'd slap you too.'

I had never seen Margherita so violent.

'Look out, there!' I exclaimed. 'If you have a Pope and a long line of Counts behind you, you must control your temper. Ancestors are a terrific responsibility.'

Then I asked her to give me the details of the story.

'It will all be cleared up soon,' she told me, 'and there'll be complete documentary proof. Then I shall call upon you for technical advice as to how to frame the parchment with my coat-of-arms.'

'Are you going to have one of those too?' I asked her.

As I looked with concern at Margherita, distant childhood memories surged up into my mind. I remembered a dusty attic, filled with bric-à-brac of every description. There were photographic enlargements of people long since dead and three coats-of-arms on imitation parchment paper, each one different from the others. Under the first, a legend in Gothic letters claimed that our family came down from a long line of prelates, soldiers and noblemen of French origin. The legend under the second made no less ambitious claims, but described the family as Portuguese, while according to the third its origins were Polish. I asked my grandfather which story was true, and I can still see him stroking his beard as he answered:

'None of them, probably. But don't let that worry you. It isn't history that counts; it's geography. If Great Britain were in Switzerland, it would never have become a great sea power.'

Now I felt worried as I looked at Margherita.

'A man came by the other day,' she explained, 'a very

earnest fellow, a scholar. He said that in the course of some historical research he had had occasion to examine my family tree and found all sorts of important people, people with titles and high military rank, yes, and even a Pope. He happened to be passing this way, and so he stopped in to tell me. Within a week he'll send me the coat-of-arms and its complete story.'

I said that I got the idea, but I advanced a few doubts as to its validity.

'Nino, there's no need to worry,' Margherita assured me. 'I'd never laid eyes on him before, and the fact that he bothered to look me up shows that he has really gone into the matter.'

Margherita's logic is unbeatable.

'I hope that you gave him an advance on the coat-of-arms and its story,' I said at last.

'Of course, I wasn't going to let a chance like that get away.'

And Margherita went off, trailing her nobility behind her. Already I could notice a change in her gait. In the following days she was in superbly good humour.

'One must never be discouraged,' she said reflectively one evening as we sat in front of the fire. 'Just when I lost faith in the future, I acquired faith in the past.'

As a general proposition, this wasn't so bad, but the trouble with Margherita is that in such cases she comes right down to concrete examples. Now we were silent for a few minutes, until she said:

'Look at the pear tree, for instance. What does the pear tree do?'

The mention of fruit trees drew Albertino and the Duchess into the conversation.

'Tell me, children,' said Margherita, 'what does the pear tree do?'

'The pear tree produces pears,' answered Albertino.

Margherita shook her head.

'Behold the pear tree!' she said with a biblical intonation. 'Your father has cut and trimmed its shoots, and now the tree is sad, because in its top branches lay all its hopes for the future. But now that its impulse to grow upward is checked, what does the pear tree do? Its roots, which no longer have such a great superstructure to nourish, grow more and more robust and suck in the life-giving lymph of the soil with greater voracity. Having lost its hope for the future, it digs deeper into the ground and centres its hopes in the past. The trunk, which represents the present, because its feet are in the past and its head in the future, draws fresh vitality, as I have said, from the earth, and as its faith in the future gradually returns, new shoots grow out of the top and rise to conquer the sky.... Mark my words, Giovannino, I feel just like that pear tree today!'

The Duchess gave signs of disapproval.

'I don't care for that story,' she said. 'It's too much like the silly things they put into school readers.'

Albertino didn't agree. He thought the story was very fine, but he didn't see why people clipped the branches of trees instead of the roots.

'When you go to the barber, does he cut your feet or your hair?' Margherita asked him.

'My hair.'

'Then why would you expect anyone to cut the feet of a tree?'

This is the kind of lesson that Margherita has a way of giving her children.

'It teaches them to reason, to proceed logically from one idea to another,' she says. 'Besides that, it sharpens their spirituality and reinforces their moral principles.'

*

For a fortnight Margherita lived off her newly recovered hope in the past. Finally she received a parcel, collect, with 8300 liras to pay. Inside was a cardboard roll containing two sheets of parchment paper. Margherita gave one of them to me, and underneath the elaborate coat-of-arms I read my own name.

'I had him look up your family too,' she told me. 'I could see that you were mortified when I told you about mine. After all, you have just as much right to a past as I have.'

With appreciation of her generosity, I plunged into what the historian had to say about my lineage. Here is what I read:

An ancient and illustrious family, which came as early as the 11th century from Spain. Marquis Joselito, a special envoy from the King of Spain to the Holy See, settled permanently in Rome in 1196. The Spanish Congress, having met in special session at the royal command, allotted the family 5000 pieces of gold and perpetual listing in the Patrician Directory. And the Holy Father awarded the Collar of the Holy Roman Empire to Domingo, First Knight of Honour of the Palatine Guard (see Ecclesiastical Papers listed in the bibliography below).'

'Aren't you happy?' Margherita asked.

'Yes, there's something I didn't know, that we had our roots in Spain. Too bad I had to find it out at a time when Barcelona is in the throes of a bus strike.'

Just then the Duchess came up and said the bird in the centre of my coat-of-arms looked like a chicken and that as for the lions, she could have drawn them better herself.

'Let's see yours, Margherita,' I put in.

When Margherita opened her roll, she found a petty affair with no decoration and the following legend:

'According to students of genealogy, this family comes from a collateral branch of the Gabutti. It held feudal possession of Bralia and of land in the region of San Romanao and the title of Count. The family story is a long one, studded with magnificent names. Arms: Party per pale, or and argent. A tree vert fourché eradicated.'

The Red Duchess said the tree was a cabbage, but Albertino called it spinach.

'The Pope isn't there, but the title of Count is all yours,' I said. 'It's fine history, in my opinion.'

But Margherita was disappointed.

'How does the Gabutto family come into it?' she asked. 'My name's about as much like Gabutto as Barigazzi is like Tellini. And if you detach a branch from the pear tree, it will always partake of the nature of pear.'

We held the parchment up to the light to examine it more

closely and under Margherita's name we found *Gabuzzi*.

'Of course Gabuzzi could come from Gabutti,' said Margherita. 'But how do you explain this mix-up?'

I threw out my arms in despair.

'It's no mix-up, Margherita,' I told her. 'Your scholarly friend sent this collect to someone called Gabuzzi, who refused to accept it. Then he covered Gabuzzi with purple ink and wrote in your name. But because he couldn't erase the India ink entirely, he put you down as belonging to a collateral branch of the Gabutti family. You see, my grandfather was right after all, when he said that geography counts much more than history.'

Margherita went to look out the window.

'Daily life is such a sordid affair,' she sighed. 'There's nothing but emptiness behind us. . . . How do you feel about it, Giovannino?'

'Now that my beginnings have been traced back to Spain as well as three other countries, I feel like a citizen of the world, that's all,' I answered.

'We're just an unfortunate generation,' Margherita concluded.

Roll-call

As I was walking rather sloppily along the former 'Imperial' avenue, stopping to look into shop windows on my way, a voice called out:

'Lieutenant!'

I turned round, and there was Calogero of the field artillery.

'The best fellow in our battery!' I exclaimed. 'And the one who was on sick leave the most often.'

'You have a good memory, sir.'

I looked at him in honest surprise, and he must have guessed the reason.

'It seems like only yesterday, Lieutenant, but it was ten years ago.'

I asked him if he was passing through Milan, and he said this had been his home for the last fifteen years.

'I've always followed your name, sir. There isn't one of your books I haven't read.'

' "Sir"!'

I noticed that he was very well dressed, in a well-cut suit, highly polished shoes, a clean shirt and matching tie, with freshly shaved cheeks and smoothly combed hair. While the lieutenant was in his shirt-sleeves, with a four-day old beard on his face and rumpled hair, wearing a check shirt, a scarf round his neck instead of a tie, a green sweater, creased, yellowish duck trousers and moccasins.

'"Lieutenant, sir"!'

I felt as if I ought to button something up, but out of the five buttons of my sweater, two were missing and the other three had sunk into the holes around them. Instead, I asked my gunner friend what sort of work he did in civilian life.

'I'm in the fruit business, sir,' he told me. 'May I send a basket of peaches to your children?'

I thanked him but said I couldn't accept the offer.

'Why not, sir?'

Why not, indeed? We talked a little longer and before we parted, I gave him my address.

'Good-bye, sir,' he said.

*

When I reached the gate of my own house, I had to ring the bell four times before anyone bothered to answer. Finally, the electrical mechanism went off, and the gate opened. Margherita was reading the adventures of Lord Lister, and did not even raise her head when I walked in. The Duchess continued to paste coloured figures into a notebook that lay across her knees, and Albertino went straight on with his water-colour. I was put out by the general indifference.

'If the cat had wandered in instead of myself, he would have made just about as much of a splash,' I grumbled.

'No,' said Margherita, with her eyes still on her reading, 'because the cat wouldn't have jabbed over and over at the bell, the way you did.'

I didn't rise to this provocation.

'I say that even the cat wouldn't have received such an impolite and disrespectful greeting. This is no way to welcome the head of the family when he comes home after a hard day's work.'

'Quite right!' said Margherita. 'From now on, there's going to be a big change.... Listen, children, because this involves you as well.... As soon as your father leaves the house, you, Duchess, will keep watch before the gate. As soon as you see him coming home, you'll call out: "Attention, guard of honour!" Then Albertino, the cat and I will line up beside the door, and when your father reaches the gate, we'll sound three blasts of the trumpet. Is that clear?'

This bit of sarcasm only depressed me.

'Margherita, today, ten years after he'd seen me for the last time, a gunner from my battery recognized me in the street and called me: "Lieutenant!"'

'What else was he to call you? He knew you as his lieutenant, didn't he?'

'Yes, he knew me as his lieutenant, but he also knows who I really am and what I do today. Meeting me in civilian clothes, ten years later, he should have called me: "Mr So-and-so." Instead of which, he called me "Lieutenant".'

'I see now,' said Margherita. 'His calling you that made you feel like a commanding officer. You mistook this house for your army barracks and began meting out discipline to all and sundry. It wasn't so far off, when I suggested a sentinel at the gate and a guard of honour. There was a military note in your voice. But don't be excited, Giovannino. Put your sword back in its sheath and return to the bosom of your family!'

Of course, Margherita hadn't understood a thing.

'I didn't bare any sword, Margherita,' I told her. 'And I'm not in the least bit excited. But in these times, when everyone's morale is so low, I must admit it gave me a jolt to be called "Lieutenant". What matters isn't so much the title he gave me as the jolt I received when I heard it.'

'Are you nostalgic for the good old days of the war?'

'It's something more than that. The war destroyed my house and all my hard-earned savings and brought sufferings upon myself and my family. I can't very well feel nostalgic about that. But after all I've gone through to rebuild what was destroyed by the war, I must admit that "Lieutenant" gave me pleasure. It means that while Nino the Citizen was doing his everyday work, Lieutenant Nino was still serving the colours. In spite of the country's spiritual demobilization, the "Lieutenant" is still on the job.'

Margherita looked at me in bewilderment.

'Giovannino, you aren't to go into those "double identities" again, are you? The "Giovannino of flesh and blood" and the "spiritual Giovannino". The "self" and the "other self". You'll persuade me that I'm married to a mob instead of a man.'

'It's all very simple, Margherita. You've married a man who hasn't deserted his duty, in spite of the dereliction around him. "Lieutenant!" someone said all of a sudden, as if he were calling the roll, and the Lieutenant answered: "Present! Here I am, in this ragbag suit, with this scarf round my neck and my handlebar moustache." I didn't know myself that the "Lieutenant" was there, and I'm happy to have discovered him.'

Margherita turned to the youth battalions.

'Children, fetch the Lieutenant's uniform from the wardrobe upstairs. The Lieutenant is off to the wars.'

I said angrily that it was no laughing matter, and when the Red Duchess asked her mother if she should bring down my old Army underwear along with the uniform, I launched into a regular sermon on children's duties towards their parents. The Duchess sat down, and as I went out of the room I heard her mumble:

'This filthy war will finish some day!'

*

That afternoon a boy brought a basket of peaches and one of grapes from Calogero.

'The fruits of profiteering no doubt!' said Margherita. I stalked indignantly out of the room and took refuge in my study, where a moment later she came to join me.

'May I speak to you, Lieutenant?' she asked. 'Or must I first come to attention?'

I didn't answer, and she went on:

'When you were a boy, Nino, you worked as doorman in a sugar factory. Now if a former employee of that factory were to come up on the street and say: "Hello, doorman!" would you get a big kick out of it?'

'No,' I answered. 'I watched over a parking-lot for bicycles once, too, and it wouldn't thrill me to be hailed

'Hello, watchman!' either. But what does that matter? I don't see any connexion with the "Lieutenant" story.'

'There is a connexion, though,' Margherita replied. 'During the war, it was your duty to be a soldier. Before that, it was your duty to function efficiently as a doorman or watchman, since this was the only honest work you could find. Today you're pleased because Lieutenant Nino answered the roll-call; you know that whenever he is needed, he will always be there. But I can't share your pleasure. I'm not convinced that Nino the doorman is as loyal as Nino the Lieutenant.'

'I don't see why Nino the doorman needs to be on the alert.'

'Because if we were to be forced out on to the street tomorrow, and the only job you could find was as a doorman, I'm not sure that you'd take it.'

'Nonsense!' I exclaimed. 'I'd have to.'

'Exactly! You'd *have* to! You'd accept it as a dirty trick on Fate's part. Whereas, if you were recalled by the army, you'd be proud of doing your duty. So you see, Giovannino, I'm pleased with the Lieutenant, but disappointed in the doorman. The doorman isn't ready to answer the roll-call; in fact, he's anxious to wriggle out of the job. The doorman is a slacker, and a slacker's even worse than a deserter.'

I didn't know what to answer. After she had gone away, I found there were still two hours before supper and went out for a quiet walk in the outskirts of the city. I was thinking about my past and my future. And all the while I looked at the green fields, stopped on the grassy bank of a stream, dipped my hand into the cool water and pinched a bit of earth between my fingers.

'They can take everything away,' I said to myself. 'They can take life itself, but they can't take my faith in life!'

I came back to the house with a great weight lifted off my chest. As soon as I turned the corner, the Duchess, who was keeping watch at the gate, shouted:

'Guard of honour, attention!'

And the guard was deployed at the door. Margherita stepped forward, saluted and said:

'Nothing new to report, sir.'

'This isn't the Lieutenant,' I told her. 'This is the doorman.'

'Good!' said Margherita. 'Even if it's only symbolical, the mobilization must be a general one. That's the way for us to win.'

Margherita is always right.

Predestined Reality

FOR a whole hour I had been trying to unravel the skein of a story that was wound up in my head, and I had just about found the loose end for which I was searching when Margherita came into the room.

'The grocer!' she said with eloquent brevity, destroying in a single second the result of all my hard work.

I made the grocer the subject of a few not very complimentary remarks, but Margherita would not be sidetracked from her purpose.

'He may be one of the lower forms of animal life,' she said, 'but he's got to be paid. Then there's the little matter of the telephone bill. And you must decide what you want to have for lunch.'

I maintained that none of these things was my concern. All my money was in her hands, and it was up to her to cook lunch.

'That doesn't matter,' said Margherita. 'It's unfair to dump all the household responsibilities on to your wife's shoulders. You owe me your moral support.'

'But, Margherita, you don't need my moral support to pay the grocery and telephone bills, do you? Haven't I done my share in very concrete form by providing the money?'

Margherita gave a long sigh.

'Money! That's all a man ever has on his mind! When you've given me the money to pay the bills, you think you've performed something over and above the call of duty. In your eyes, the house is a business proposition. And I say that if a house is to be a home, then it entails the day-by-day creation of predestined reality.'

The whole thing seemed to me like a contradiction in terms.

'Margherita,' I tried to explain, 'to apply oneself day by day to the creation of predestined reality is like saying: "Today is Tuesday. Let's figure out what day it will be tomorrow, Wednesday." Because, according to plan, Wednesday, Thursday, Friday follow in inevitable succession.'

'With Barilla spaghetti, every meal is a Sunday dinner!' said the Duchess as she came into the room.

But Margherita was not discouraged either by my logic or the Duchess' sarcasm.

'If there's such a thing as fate,' she insisted, 'then everything in the world is predestined reality. Everything goes like Monday-Tuesday-Wednesday. But only sticks and stones are supine enough to accept the reality that's been planned for them. Man is master, not victim of his fate. Man isn't like the hand of a watch, which goes from four to five o'clock just because predestined reality and the passage of time compel it to do so. Yes, man *is* like the hand of a clock, if you like, but he is a *reasoning* hand. He goes from four to five o'clock because he *understands* that the reality planned for him demands it and it is his inescapable duty to make this reality come to pass, or in other words to create it.'

It was the word *inescapable* that annoyed me most, especially in view of the fact that the hands of the clock on my desk were working hard to create the inescapable reality of eleven a.m.

'Margherita, we've got to put this straight,' I told her. 'Here is the situation. On the days when I potter about the house, dig in the garden or just stretch out in an armchair and whistle, nobody ever disturbs me. But as soon as I settle down to work, people fire questions at me and compel me to listen to theories as wild as the one you have just put forward. Just look: your son has wormed his way into the room, and now all that's missing is the cat. Now tell me:

can you explain the logic of this predestined reality which you create to my detriment every time I start working?'

Margherita did not yield an inch.

'You wouldn't expect me to disturb your rest, would you, Giovannino? When you've finished your work and have a sacred right to repose. And by respecting your rest, I respect your work as well.'

The confusion of this statement left me gaping, and Albertino took advantage of my silence to say that the plumber, carpenter, mason and cabinet-maker were all awaiting my instructions downstairs. Apparently they had the same principles about disturbing my rest as Margherita.

I decided to go back to working at night, after everyone else had gone to bed, the way I had done as a cub reporter on a provincial newspaper. Life begins at forty. I worked quietly for three nights in succession, and every morning, as soon as I heard the rest of the family getting up, I went to bed. But the fourth night, just as I was getting up steam, Margherita appeared at my study door.

'The awnings,' she shot at me.

It didn't take me long to find out that Margherita wasn't walking in her sleep but meant serious business.

'We simply must decide what colour we want the awnings and how we are to install them,' was what she had to say.

Obviously, she was intent upon creating predestined reality again. We talked about the awnings for a while and then went into the important question of the refrigerator. Finally I said to Margherita:

'Why, in heaven's name, did you come here at two o'clock in the morning to discuss these things? Couldn't you have gone on sleeping?'

'I couldn't possibly sleep,' she told me, with emotion in her voice. 'I heard you tapping away on your machine and my conscience wouldn't let me rest.'

'Look here, Margherita,' I said gently. 'How could you hear me tapping on the typewriter when for the last four days it's been undergoing repairs, and I've had to write with a pen.'

163

'Then tonight you must be very heavy-handed,' Margherita said calmly.

At about three o'clock the Duchess came to find out if she could use the paint brush in the garage to touch up her bicycle. Then at a quarter past four, Albertino popped in to ask whether or not Pancho Villa was a real person. At half past four, the cat began to meow in a most atrocious manner.

Things went on this way for several nights in succession and I couldn't afford to waste time, because I had to meet a deadline. And so after some thought, I decided to retire to my shack in the country. It was scorchingly hot out there, but I didn't mind that. It meant that I should have to go on working at night, but at the same time, I should enjoy the most perfect peace and quiet that anyone can imagine.

It was in this isolated spot that I sat down to work that first evening. I typed a dozen or so lines and then stopped. Everything was still and silent; not a rustle was to be heard. When I started typing again, it was like a volley of machine-gun bullets. I wished someone would walk down the road, that a dog would bark or a chair squeak. I didn't have the courage to strike another key.

'If I touch one again, the shock will make the house tremble.'

I sat there, stock-still, listening to my heart pound, my bones creak and my breath wheeze in the silence.

'I'm going to hear everything,' I said to myself. 'The workings of my brain and the course of the blood through my arteries.'

I tried to get up, but the scraping of the chair paralysed me, and I quickly sat down.

'Nobody will come before sunrise,' I thought. 'And I shan't be able to get up, for lack of any human sound.'

At two o'clock I was still in the same state, and I had no hope of going to sleep because the buzz of my blood was unbearable. At a quarter past two, I heard a noise which froze me from head to foot. But I pulled myself together and ran into the hall. The telephone was ringing and I feverishly grasped the receiver.

'The carpeting for the stairs!' said Margherita's voice categorically. 'We must lay it down, or the steps will be ruined.'

We talked first about the carpet and then about the necessity of new soles for the shoes of Albertino. Then I went back to my typewriter and cheerfully started to work. I knew the telephone was going to ring again. It rang at three o'clock, because the Duchess wanted to know where I had left the glue. And at three-thirty because Albertino wanted to tell me the Duchess had taken it.

The next day I returned home and went back to my day schedule. The family continues to respect my rest and disturb my work, but at least I can keep on working.

Greater Love hath No Cat

I STAYED for a fortnight in Milan and when I came back to our house in the country, Margherita greeted me with:

'How's the little family?'

'You know more about that than I do. You've been running the family since I went away.'

'I'm not referring to *this* family,' Margherita explained. 'I mean your *other* family, the new family you've set up for yourself in Milan.'

I said I wasn't in a joking mood, but Margherita shrugged her shoulders.

'How do I know?' she said. 'I hear people say that all the time you were there, you couldn't answer the telephone or even write a letter, because you'd set up housekeeping and your "wife" had you under her thumb. . . .'

I told her that any man who has a mere fortnight to do all the work that I had found waiting for me in the city must be forgiven for not wasting time over personal letters and telephone calls. Margherita only sighed and did not pursue the argument.

But, to tell you the truth, I hadn't done a single stroke of work in Milan. I had spent the whole time sleeping, reading and messing about with old papers. And waiting for the ground sausage to be finished. Because my stay in the city hadn't to do with business at all; it was simply a very urgent matter of sausage meat. An enormous quantity of ground sausage had come into my life, upon which peace and quiet had gone out the window and the future was overhung by a great black cloud.

*

One evening at supper the idea of country sausage swam into my mind.

'Cornmeal and sausage!' I exclaimed. 'That's what I crave!'

'We'll have them tomorrow,' Margherita assured me.

But the next day we had neither one nor the other, and I had to remind Margherita of her promise. The day after that we spoke of them at both lunch and supper, for the very simple reason that neither was on the table. And the following day it was the same story all over again.

'Cornmeal and sausage! Cornmeal and sausage!' Margherita exclaimed. 'Haven't you anything else on your mind? We can't go on eating cornmeal and sausage for the rest of our lives!'

As usual, Margherita had passed from the defence to the attack, and now she had the effrontery to present herself as a victim to the public eye. It was no use arguing with so treacherous an opponent, so I decided to take action. The next day I went to see my friend Augusto.

'I'd like you to slaughter a hog,' I told him.

'Just leave it to me. I've got just the hog for you, and also a man to prepare the meat. How do you want it cut?'

'He can cut it any way he likes. What interests me is sausage. It's a matter of principle. For a month now I've been asking my wife for a half-pound of ground sausage, and she hasn't done anything about it. Now I'm going to inflict it upon her by the carload. Let your butcher grind as much as he can. Refinement isn't the object; as I said before, there's a principle involved.'

And so we struck up an agreement. Augusto would slaughter a hog, have it cut up and hung by his butcher and send me the largest possible quantity of ground sausage. I went back home feeling quite pleased with myself and didn't open my mouth on the subject of my craving. After five or six days had gone by, Augusto called me up to say that 'he had found the book I wanted to borrow', and I dashed right over to his house in my car.

First Augusto took me into the kitchen to show me the strings of *salame*, and expounded his idea of exactly what type was best suited to a family of the size and character of mine. He was just about to tell me about the meat that was still soaking in brine, when I interrupted him with:

'The ground sausage!'

Whereupon he took me down into the cellar. Few of my readers can have an idea of how much sausage meat can be obtained by dint of concentrated effort from a single six hundred and fifty pound hog. Before I saw this gigantic cube of sausage, I hadn't the remotest notion myself. To make a long story short, just imagine a granite block measuring 25 × 20 × 8 inches. But please remember that granite is one thing and sausage is another, and one infinitely more difficult to digest. In any case, I picked up the cube and put it in the luggage compartment of my car. When I reached home I left the car near the kitchen door, got out and hung about with apparent indifference until it was time for supper. Luck was with me, for what should appear on the supper table but a dish of yellow cornmeal, as big and round as a harvest moon.

'At last,' I exclaimed. 'Tonight we'll have cornmeal and fresh sausage.'

Margherita threw me an almost suspicious look.

'Are we going to start that again?' she asked. 'If you wanted sausage, you should have let me know.'

'It's cornmeal and sausage tonight!' I repeated joyfully.

Of course I had arranged everything in advance, and the second time I said the word 'cornmeal' was the cue for Albertino and the Duchess to come in, bearing the sausage block on a gigantic platter. I put the platter in the centre of the table, and it was so impressively monumental, that Margherita stared at it with amazement and something close to fear.

We stuffed ourselves with cornmeal and sausage, and Margherita was too crushed to utter a single word. The next day we had cornmeal and sausage for both lunch and dinner, and the next day after that too. I held out for four days more. But at that point, when I saw the sausage block appear on the table, I started to say:

'After all . . .'

Margherita shot me an atomic look.

'There you are!' she shouted. 'When there's no sausage he makes it into a tragedy, and when there is sausage, that's a tragedy too. Would you please tell me what you want?'

I said that I hadn't made it into a tragedy at all, and had no intention of doing so. My 'after all' was apropos of something that had no connexion with sausage meat whatsoever.

'"After all" is an exclamation suited to the first sight of Niagara Falls or the Aurora Borealis,' I told her, 'but before a noble pile of sausage meat, there's really nothing to say.'

Margherita regained her good humour and ate up her lunch. The day after that, when I failed to pronounce the words 'cornmeal and sausage' at either lunch or supper, Margherita remarked happily:

'Giovannino, you'll never know how glad I am to have found something you really like.'

All night long I turned the problem over in my mind. I calculated the weight of the ground sausage that still remained and pitted it against the capacities of Margherita, the Duchess, Albertino, Giacomina, and the maid. Finally I came to this conclusion:

'If I leave for Milan tomorrow morning and stay away for a fortnight, then the sausage will be finished by the time I get back.'

No sooner said than done. I frittered away my time in Milan, and then came home, feeling quite cocky about myself and my future. I wandered around the house, testing locks and faucets, and finally took a casual look at the supplies in the food cupboard. The cube of sausage meat was still there, just as I had left it a fortnight before. I shuddered with horror. Just then the Red Duchess came into the cupboard in order to cut herself a slice of cheese.

'Haven't you had any ground sausage since I've been away?' I asked her with studied indifference.

'No,' said the Duchess. 'We wanted to have some, but Mother said you liked it so much that we ought to leave it for you. So after that we never touched it. If a father has a taste for something, then his children must give it up and eat something else instead.'

I had to applaud this self-sacrificing spirit.

'You really should have eaten it, though,' I told her. 'Because sausage meat doesn't keep. It's probably spoiled by now.'

'No,' said the Duchess. 'Mother telephoned Signor Augusto, and he said that in this cool weather it would keep for at least a month.'

'Good!' I said gaily, but with my heart in my boots. 'But instead of eating cheese for your afternoon snack, you may just as well cut yourself a slice of sausage.'

The Duchess shook her head.

'Oh no,' she said. 'That's yours, all of it. But perhaps we might have a slice for supper.'

Merciful Heaven! Was supper going to be cornmeal and sausage? I returned to wandering around the house, and at a certain point I picked up the cat, locked him in the cupboard and put the key in my pocket. An hour later, I came back to see what progress he had made. The cat hadn't so much as touched the sausage, and when I took him by the nape of his neck and held him close to it, he meowed in fear.

I decided to call upon some less stupid felines, and so I opened the window, put some pieces of meat on the sill and then hopefully closed the cupboard door behind me. Our house is commonly held – and with reason – to be the mecca of all the cats of the neighbourhood. And these cats are of a wildly hungry tribe, so bold that once upon a time when one of them got through the cupboard window, he tried to open a tin of condensed milk with his claws and very nearly succeeded. Now, looking out into the courtyard, I saw the cats arriving with as much alacrity as if they had received a radio mobilization order. I went up to the second floor, but a few minutes later there was such pandemonium below that I had to come back downstairs, where I found Margherita looking desperately for the cupboard key.

'I slipped it into my pocket without thinking,' I told her as I handed it over.

She disappeared, but a few minutes later she called to me from the cupboard. I went to join her, and immediately she said, pointing to the floor:

'Just look at that, will you!'

I had never seen a cat reduced to such a condition, and for a moment I couldn't believe that it was ours.

'Just look at him, Giovannino,' she added. 'Some careless fool opened this window and forgot to close it. An army of robber cats tried to take the place by storm, but ours stood on guard. They were ten to one, but a cat with such a sense of duty knows no fear. He fought like a lion, without ever yielding an inch. The claws of his assailants tore his tender flesh, but he never gave in. There he is, bloody but unbowed, triumphant over all his foes! And his master's beloved sausage is safe from the invaders. Safe and whole! Safe and pure! For they were not able so much as to graze it. Look at him, Nino, and tell me if he isn't a hero to have risked his life for his master's favourite meat!'

I bent over to stroke the head of the heroic cat, and whispered into his ear:

'You villain!'

No, I am not afraid to write these words. Let the Society for the Prevention of Cruelty to Animals say what it will! I shall not hesitate to repeat what I said then: 'This cat is no hero. He's a miserable villain!' If the Society for the Prevention of Cruelty to Animals had a conscience, it would protect me and not my cat. For the cat didn't have to eat cornmeal and sausage that evening.

Yes, that evening I ate cornmeal and sausage, and I ate them alone, because the others wouldn't deprive me of a single morsel and insisted on sacrificing themselves for my benefit. I ate them that evening and many evenings to come; in fact I am eating them still. And I cannot say a word, lest Margherita accuse me of ingratitude towards my devoted wife, children and cat.

Yes, I am the hero of the story! Greater love hath no cat than this! And my victory is far more heroic than the one

I have just recounted. For single-handed I have encompassed and destroyed the block of ground sausage, and this evening my task is done. I know that the end is at hand, For I flung my challenge to high heaven and now no hand but that of God can stop me.

It's the Principle that Matters

IT happened in the usual way. I left home, went to the nearest taxi-rank, climbed into a cab, then had to give my home address instead of that of the office. When we reached the gate of my house I asked the driver to wait while I rang the bell and called out to my wife:

'Margherita, please give me my wallet.'

And, as usual, Margherita shot me a look of annoyance from the top step, went into the house and then reappeared. Only this time she didn't have my wallet in her hand.

'It isn't here,' she said; 'you must have it yourself.'

But I was quite sure of the contrary.

'You must have forgotten to put it back where it belongs,' I said ironically.

'I always keep everything in its proper place,' she retorted.

'Everything except my wallet,' I insisted, 'And after I've left the house and started off in a tram or taxi to the office I suddenly realize that my wallet is missing and have to come back for it. If you ask me, you really ought to stop lifting it out of my pocket.'

Margherita shook her head.

'When I need money for food, where am I supposed to get it? From the priest? If you didn't want to support a family, you should never have married.'

I was standing on the pavement, clasping the iron bars of the gate.

'Listen, Margherita,' I said, 'I only mean that when you want money you ought to ask me for it instead of taking it away.'

'You don't trust me, is that it?' exclaimed Margherita in an injured tone of voice. 'You want to check and double-check, I see. You don't think I'm capable of running the house. Or perhaps you imagine that I'm piling up bills at the most expensive shops, or putting your money into a secret bank account I have opened in my own name!'

'Margherita, I don't want to check and doublecheck at all. I simply want to avoid being stuck in a tram, taxi or café without a penny in my pocket. . . . Meanwhile, *where* is my wallet?'

'I can't imagine where you put it,' she countered. 'I've looked all over the place without success. Try to remember, Nino.'

I remembered only that my wallet was in my pocket when I returned to the house the night before and that I hadn't touched it between then and now.

'Margherita, when I was working in my study this morning, didn't you have any occasion to pay some tradesman's bill?'

'No, not a soul came to the house, not the baker, the butcher, the grocer . . . I remember perfectly.'

For some months a group of masons had been adding extra floors to the house next door, and now one of them peered over the dividing wall and said:

'Lady, the shoemaker's boy came to your house this morning and I heard you say: "Wait a minute and I'll pay you for the soles."'

'That's not so,' said Margherita; 'he came yesterday.'

'The lady's right,' shouted the foreman from the top of his ladder. 'The shoemaker's boy came yesterday. This morning it was the collector from the gas company.'

The two men entered into a lively argument, which ended in a compromise. It was agreed that the visitor in question was the milkman.

'Do you remember that you asked me if I could change a five-thousand lira bill?' said the carpenter, who was by now a third party to the discussion. Margherita assumed a puzzled look, but she took this blow on the chin.

'Right you are!' she admitted. 'But after I had paid the milkman I remember distinctly putting the wallet back into my husband's pocket. After that, as usual, he took it out and tucked it away, God knows where.'

'I didn't budge from the house all morning,' I reminded her. 'How could I have taken it out of my pocket?'

Margherita gave me a condescending smile.

'The devil finds work for idle hands to do,' she observed.

I couldn't argue with her on this point, so I strove to maintain my self-control.

'Margherita, it's not a question of placing the blame,' I told her. 'We've simply got to find the wallet. You're sure that you put it back in my pocket, and I'm convinced that I never took it out. If we both maintain these intransigent positions, the wallet will never be found.'

'Well, what next?' asked Margherita suspiciously.

'We must both abandon our extremes and admit that there is a chance of our having made a mistake. I'll admit to start with that I may have removed the wallet from my pocket and put it God knows where.'

Margherita came out with a fatuous smile.

'I knew it would come to that,' she said, 'because I'm absolutely positive that I put the wallet back in your jacket.'

Margherita had struck below the belt and I smarted from her blow.

'There's a pretty state of affairs!' I shouted. 'When I'm as reasonable as anyone can be, you turn on me with un-reason! If I admit that in a moment of distraction I may have taken the wallet out of my pocket, why can't you confess the possibility of your making a mistake too?'

'Why not indeed!' said Margherita serenely. 'When you're drawing near to the truth, why should I turn you away? You took the wallet yourself; now just try to remember where you put it.'

Things had come to such a pass that I couldn't go on indefinitely hanging on to the bars. I asked Margherita to open the gate and let me in. But the quarrel had gone so far that even if we were to have carried it on within the four walls of the house, people could have followed it from the outside. In order to find support for her cause, Margherita turned to the Red Duchess:

'Tell your father where I put his wallet after I took the money for the milkman!'

But the Duchess only shook her head.

'Money business doesn't concern me,' she said.

'Listen to that!' shouted Margherita, who was beside herself. 'Don't you know it's your duty to stand up for your mother?'

'I didn't see a thing,' maintained the Red Duchess. 'Let everyone stick to his own business, that's what I say.'

Margherita looked at her with disgust. She proceeded to question Albertino, but he claimed to be equally in the dark. Finally Margherita threw herself into a chair.

'Three to one!' she sobbed. 'My own children have turned against me!' Then she recovered her aplomb and said harshly: 'I don't need any help! I have confidence in myself, that is my vindication. If the wallet is missing, you must have taken it. The very fact that you admit such a possibility is proof enough. As for me, I'm not admitting a thing!'

The affair was taking a more and more dramatic turn, but I had a limited objective in view, namely to recover my wallet.

'Margherita,' I said with all the patience at my command, 'admit for the sake of sheer absurdity that you didn't put the wallet back in my pocket, and ...'

'Absurdity is the negation of truth,' Margherita answered severely, 'and truth is like a crystal block. To say that truth isn't true is like cracking the crystal. Truth isn't something than can be denied; it's something to be defended!'

The argument became engulfed in these abstract terms until I said firmly:

'I want my wallet! Let everyone get to work looking

for it right away! I won't stand for any more discussion.'

Margherita looked at me mistrustfully.

'We'll look,' she said, 'and if we're successful it will be found just where you left it!'

A systematic search was begun and went on for the next twenty minutes. In the course of the twenty-first minute I found the wallet myself, locked in a desk drawer, where only I could have put it, since the key was on my key-chain. Margherita stared at me for some time without speaking, then, pointing her forefinger in my direction, she said to the children:

'There's your father for you! You can judge him for yourselves.'

'The triumph of innocence!' Albertino said gravely.

The Duchess preferred to remain noncommittal.

'I'm sorry, Margherita,' I said in deep humiliation. 'But the wallet is found, and that's the most important thing after all.'

I stepped into the garden for a breath of fresh air, and suddenly realized that the taxi was still waiting for me in front of the gate.

'Good Lord, I forgot all about you,' I said to the driver. 'Tell me how much I owe you and run along. I'm not going anywhere for the moment.'

'You don't owe me a thing,' he answered. 'I stayed to find out what would happen. You found it, didn't you?'

'Yes,' I said throwing out my arms helplessly.

'Where was it?'

'Locked up in one of my desk drawers. And I must have put it there, because the key is in my pocket.'

The driver brought his fist down on the steering-wheel.

'Damn it! That's something I never expected. I'd have sworn your wife was guilty.'

'Well, I'm the guilty one, unfortunately. I'm losing my memory, that's all.'

Just then someone tugged at my jacket, and turning around I saw it was the Duchess.

'It wasn't in your desk at all,' she said in a low voice. 'It was in *her* handbag. So I took it and put it in the drawer.'

I was completely taken aback.

'What about the key?' I stammered. 'How could you have put it in the drawer when I had the key?'

'I have a copy of that myself,' she said, holding it up for me to see.

'Well, well, well!' exclaimed the driver. 'I had a hunch your wife was wrong. Now it's up to you to enjoy your triumph.'

The Duchess was looking up into the air, and I said to the taxi-driver:

'Let's leave things the way they are. I'll pretend I don't know any more than I did before.'

The driver twirled his grey moustache.

'Well, perhaps you're right,' he admitted. 'The essential victory is ours, the principle of the thing is all that really matters.'

He slipped the taxi into gear and drove off at full speed, shouting over his shoulder:

'What can a fellow do? He just has to grin and bear it!'

I looked hard at the Duchess, who finally shrugged her shoulders and said:

'After all, I'm the daughter of both of you!'

There she was right. Of course there was still the question of why she should have a duplicate key. But that was a mere detail, and I decided to overlook it.

The Favourite Present

THE doorbell kept ringing, and every time it was a messenger or delivery boy with a telegram, a bunch of flowers or a parcel of some kind. It wouldn't have been in keeping with the dignity of the occasion for the Duchess to answer, and so she simply waited for Albertino to bring back whatever the gift might be.

The Duchess has a definite personality and is in complete command of all of her few years. She has tiny bones and if you could see her it wouldn't surprise you to hear that on the day of her birth she weighed no more than three and a half pounds. On the November day in 1943 when we took her to be christened, the gigantic priest who was officiating said to Margherita as he took her tiny bundle into his arms: 'It looks as if you made the least possible effort!'

She has tiny bones, as I say, and a proportionately small body, but her personality is another matter. 'She knows how to hold up her cards,' as they say in my part of the country about a woman possessed of unusual self-control. And so it is easy to imagine how controlled she was on such a special day as that of her First Communion. She wore her white dress with impressive dignity, and her every gesture was in tune with the austerity of what she was wearing. And every time the doorbell rang, she waited for the return of Albertino.

Flowers, telegrams and presents of every description,

including a magnificent calico doll, which aroused the enthusiasm of Margherita, but left the recipient unmoved in spite of the pleasure it must have given her. When it comes to her wedding, and the Duchess is asked whether or not she takes the young man beside her for her husband, she will doubtless answer: 'I suppose so,' in an exceedingly casual manner.

Now, at any rate, she greeted every gift with the briefest possible acknowledgment of its arrival and the most restrained enjoyment, as expressed in a laconic: 'Very nice!' or 'Very pretty!'

Margherita was vexed by her indifference.

'People have put themselves out to send you the most wonderful presents, and you can't even be bothered to smile!'

The Duchess was not in the least taken aback.

'People always give you things they like themselves,' she observed. 'Let them be the ones to smile.'

At bottom, the Duchess is always right, even when she's wrong completely. Everyone that buys a present chooses what he likes best and gives the greater part of the pleasure to himself. Because the real fun lies not in receiving or making use of a present, but in being able to buy it. Now the Duchess consented munificently to receive all the things that were offered her, without batting an eyelash. Just when it seemed as if nothing else could possibly arrive, an enormous crate was brought in, which required a hammer and pincers to open. Out of the wrapping paper and excelsior appeared a shiny light blue bicycle. All turned instinctively to catch the reaction of the Red Duchess. As she stared at its shiny paint and gleaming chromium, we felt sure she would descend from her pedestal and act like a normal human being. And indeed her face did first grow pale and then regain its colour, while her lips trembled and there was a spark in her eyes.

'Surely she'll jump and shout over that,' we were all thinking.

But all she said as she sank back into her chair, was:

'It's a Legnano. Has it got a bell?'

Albertino rang the bell for an answer.

'Good,' said the Red Duchess dispassionately.

This was something, to be sure, but nothing like what we had expected. Margherita was increasingly angry.

'If she were my daughter,' she whispered to me excitedly, 'I know exactly what I'd do.'

'She *is* your daughter, Margherita,' I answered.

'No, she isn't ours today,' said Margherita. 'Today she belongs to another world.'

This seemed to be the last of the presents. The Red Duchess continued to sit in an armchair and to drop an occasional word to the people around her. Her words were short and staccato, and seemed to descend from an eighteenth storey, words that had been released in the air and now floated down as tremulously as the dead leaves of an autumn tree. This only augmented Margherita's vexation.

'Pretty soon, one will have to make a written application for an audience,' she whispered into my ear. 'Do you want to see me lift up her train and give her a good spanking?'

'If you like,' I agreed.

But I didn't see anything of the sort. Margherita did go over to the Red Duchess and touch her train, but it was only in order to eliminate a wrinkle. The Duchess thanked her with a barely perceptible nod and Margherita flushed with as much pleasure as if she had been named lady-in-waiting to the queen.

Things were at this point when the doorbell rang again and Albertino went to answer. A moment later he came back highly excited and dragging a crate the same size as the one that had enveloped the bicycle. The Red Duchess deigned to turn her head. Plainly, this business of receiving presents was becoming a bore, but she felt she couldn't detach herself from it altogether. Albertino had the energy and enthusiasm of a whole crew of wreckers, and in no time at all he had shattered the crate and strewn the excelsior all over the floor. Out came a strange green contraption with yellow trimmings. No one could make out what it was, until I shook off the shreds of wrapping that still clung to it and examined it in the light of day.

'What in heaven's name can it be?' asked Margherita.

'A bottle-corking machine,' I explained. 'What I can't fathom is why anyone should have sent it.'

'Plenty of your friends fancy themselves as wits,' Margherita said disgustedly. 'It must be that poor fool Gigi or Brogetto.'

'Signor Carletto perhaps . . .' put in Albertino.

Margherita was positively furious.

'It would be very funny if only adults were concerned,' she said. 'But to trick a little girl on her First Communion Day is not only idiotic, it's vulgar as well. There's no reason why the father's sins should be visited upon his children.'

Bolstered up by the agreement of all those present, Margherita ran to the telephone. But when she came back, she said:

'Gigi and Brogetto swear they had nothing to do with it. It must be Carletto. Only he isn't home.'

'I'm right here,' said Carletto, 'but I swear I'm not guilty. I gave her a sewing-kit – there it is on the table.'

'Somebody did it, though,' Margherita insisted. And drawing us into a corner she whispered excitedly: 'For heaven's sake, do something, all of you. Try to distract her, and explain it was all a mistake. Don't you know she's a very sensitive child? It must be one of her father's political enemies who's responsible for this cruel trick. But it may leave an indelible scar on her childish memory. We must all go into action at once.'

We were perfectly willing to try, but it was already too late. The Duchess stood in front of the outrageous machine, studying it carefully. When I walked over to her she stared me straight in the eye, and my heart turned right over. All the others were quiet, as if they were conscious of the anxiety in her stare.

'What's it for?' asked the Red Duchess, with a catch in her voice.

'What's what for?' I countered, trying to gain time.

'This wire with a metal seal on it.'

'That's a guarantee that it's brand new. It means that no one has monkeyed with the mechanism since it was tested at the factory and found to be in perfect working order.'

'How does it work?' she asked.

I broke the sealed wire.

'You raise the lever, fit a cork into this hole and then lower the lever, thereby introducing the cork into the neck of the bottle.'

'Can a cork that big be introduced into the neck of an ordinary bottle?' she said with amazement. 'I'd like to see it done.'

I ransacked the drawer of the kitchen table and found several new corks, which I moistened with olive oil. Then I brought three empty bottles up from the cellar. I placed one of the bottles in the correct position, held firm by a wooden brace, then I fitted a cork into the hole and pressed down hard upon the lever. Until this moment the Red Duchess had maintained her ethereal and detached air. But when she saw the cork actually introduced into the bottle neck, she seemed to be deeply disturbed and asked me to repeat the operation with another bottle.

'Is it very hard to do?' she asked excitedly.

'Easy as pie,' I answered, as I gave her another demonstration.

And she corked the third bottle herself, without any assistance.

'I want to do some more!' she exclaimed feverishly.

I sent out for five hundred corks and enlisted all the strong arms present to bring up two hundred empty wine bottles from the cellar.

'Just let me take your dress off,' said Margherita to her daughter.

'No, no! I've got work to do,' said the Red Duchess impatiently.

With every cork her enthusiasm increased, and after she had done twenty bottles she was shouting and laughing with joy. Albertino and the other brats were quick to organize an assembly line, but the Duchess remained in charge of the main operation. Finally we grown-ups were fed up with the whole thing and went away. While the assembly line filled the whole house with noise, the telephone rang.

'It's the man that delivered the machine,' Margherita reported. 'He says he made a mistake in the address, and he's coming to take it back. But he'll bring the tricycle or whatever it is he was originally supposed to deliver here in the first place.'

I took the receiver out of her hand.

'No,' I said. 'Everything's all right the way it is. If the man who was expecting the corking machine won't accept the tricycle in its place, then I'll send him a duplicate within the next few days.'

Half an hour later an extremely nervous individual rang up.

'I ordered that bottle-corking machine,' he shouted, 'and I want to have it right away.'

'You'll have exactly the same thing tomorrow. Or if you prefer, I'll pay you for it in cash immediately. I'll even pay more than it cost you. This one is just the thing for my little girl, who's just made her First Communion.'

'What does a First Communion have to do with it?' the individual shouted. 'I'll report you to the police.'

Margherita snatched the receiver out of my hand.

'Shame on you!' she said with a quaver in her voice. 'Shame on you for disturbing a sacred occasion! If you're an atheist or Communist or priest-hater of one kind or another, please don't choose this house for a display of your anti-clerical violence.'

She was silent for a moment, listening to his reply, and then hung up the receiver.

'What did he say?' I asked her.

'He said that he's the priest in charge of a parish nearby. Then he calmed down. He must have realized that his attitude was indefensible.'

The bottle-corking operation continued until late that night, and every bottle in the house was properly fitted, including my bottle of India ink. I don't know how they did it, but they even managed to cork the barrels of my shotgun. Before going to bed, I looked into the Duchess' room. She was fast asleep, with the machine at the foot of her bed and her white dress lying across it. The effect was nothing less than surrealistic. All the other presents were piled up in disorder, but this one was the uncontested favourite. I leaned over and whispered into her ear:

'When you marry, I'll give you a lathe or a cement-mixer.'

And she must have understood, for her lips moved in a smile.

A Christmas Present for an Overgrown Boy

'Don't forget the Christmas presents,' said Margherita, just as I was starting off to Milan. 'And remember I want them to make a big splash.'

'I'll do my very best to please the children,' I reassured her.

'Never mind about the children,' Margherita explained. 'It's *my* present that's on my mind.'

I admitted to being quite in the dark, and Margherita had to explain further.

'While you're at it, Giovannino, you may as well buy the present I want to give you. You can't say no to that. In the first place, you have more imagination than I have, and in the second, you know your own tastes much better.'

I felt deeply humiliated.

'Look here, Margherita,' I protested, 'what meaning can there be in a present I give myself?'

'You're not giving it to yourself at all! It's my present, and you're simply acting as my agent in the choice.'

It seemed to me that Margherita's laziness had gone entirely too far, and I cut her short with:

'Very well, then. I'll do without a present from you, that's all.'

'Whatever you say!' Margherita retorted. 'If you don't like my present, you're free to refuse it.'

There was no point to prolonging the argument, so I got

into the car and drove away. And after I had attended to the regular business which had brought me to the city, I started looking for presents.

*

When you're up against the job of buying an assortment of presents for people of different ages and sex, then to my mind there's only one method of attack, and that is to go to a big store, where under one roof you can find anything from toys to overcoats, from Persian rugs to transparent, illuminated globe maps of the world, from shotguns to armchairs, from andirons to bicycles, each category displayed in its own department and under the care of competent clerks.

In the early afternoon, I went to such a store and followed the procedure I have always found most efficient in a case of this kind. That is, I went calmly from one department to another, jotting down notes about everything that appealed to me on my way. After I had passed all the principal departments in review, I looked over my notes and tried to assign these various objects to the people on my Christmas list. Only when I got to this particular point, I found that none of the objects which had caught my eye was suitable to any one of the beneficiaries.

So I had recourse to another, really foolproof system; that is, I went through every department with one particular person in mind. For instance, the Duchess, my daughter. And after I had covered the whole store in this fashion, I started out again, this time with my mind on Albertino, my son.

By the end of the afternoon I had got to the bottom of my list and found I had bought the following things: three doormats, two pairs of andirons, a set of kitchen knives, a small green rug, a dozen flowered china soup bowls, a clothes-brush, an umbrella stand and several ashtrays.

The next day I came back and adopted procedure number three, which consists of trusting God and following the crowd from one counter to the next. This leads to the discovery of all sorts of new and wonderful things and unexpected answers to the most difficult problems. So that, on the day after, I had only to repeat the process once more in order to make the number of presents tally with the number of names on my list. I heaved a sigh of relief. Thank God, that was over with! It wasn't, though, because all of a sudden I remembered Margherita.

*

I had presents for everybody, yes, everybody but myself. And if I wanted to receive a present from Margherita, it was up to me to do something about it. Did I really have to bother with such foolishness?

'Whatever you say,' Margherita had told me. 'If you don't like my present, you're free to refuse it.'

And the sadness of her voice had made it seem as if my failure to buy a present for myself would be really tantamount to turning down a present she had bought for me. I was sitting meditatively over a cup of coffee and watching the crowd go by, when a thought flashed across my mind. 'What would Margherita have chosen, if she had set out to buy something for me?'

I left the café and started wandering along the street, looking into shop windows. Very soon I had the answer. Margherita would have bought me a tie. Of course! Although she knows perfectly well that I never wear a tie, that is what she would have bought. Don't women always think of a present to a man in terms of ties? But Margherita is a woman of a very unusual sort. Her illogical logic's a clear proof of that. No, she wouldn't have bought me a tie. She'd have bought me a barometer!

A barometer! That was a good joke! Why should she buy me a barometer? Except for one particular kind, where a girl with an umbrella pops out every time it's supposed to rain, barometers have never attracted me. But this one particular kind has its appeal, and I was forced to admit it. I'd wanted one for years, without a ghost of a chance of seeing it come my way.

What a lot of things I wanted when I was a child! But my family didn't give presents in those days. In fact, I never got a present at all until I bought it for myself. My mother would have liked to give me one, I knew that, but she simply couldn't. And when I finally got a bicycle, something that was just as necessary to me as my daily bread, I felt as if it had come to me from my mother.

Of course, this business with Margherita was a different story. Margherita wouldn't give me a gadget with a girl that pops out every time it's supposed to rain. Margherita is far more generous than that. I stared into one window after another, trying to figure out what in the world Margherita *would* give me. Then it came to me. That vest-pocket radio! There was the solution! I went into the shop to ask how much it cost, and then imagined the face Margherita would make when she heard the answer. The price was sky-high, and I could just hear Margherita conducting the transaction.

'*Forty thousand, did you say?*'

'*Yes, forty thousand, plus the luxury tax.*'

'*All right,*' Margherita would say calmly. '*Let's make it thirty thousand, and that's all there is to it.*'

The shopkeeper would look at her with mirthful amazement.

'*Forty thousand, and I'll absorb the tax,*' he would counter. '*But that's as far as I can go.*'

'*Then I'd better look just down the street, where I saw the same thing for thirty-two thousand.*'

I could picture the whole scene, and hear every blow struck by either side. At a certain point the shopkeeper would say in a very special tone of voice:

'*Thirty-five!*'

From his tone of voice, Margherita would understand that thirty-five thousand was the rock bottom price, and she would take the money out of her bag.

Now, I went out of the shop, imagining how Margherita would walk home, mumbling to herself:

'*If the silly man doesn't like his present, then he's out of luck!*'

I stopped to look at a window where there was a big box of tiny plastic blocks, enough of them to fit one on top of another and make a perfect little toy house. Margherita would look at it the same way and say to herself:

'*I'll get this for him, too. Just the sort of stupid thing he's sure to like.*'

Then, once she had bought the blocks, Margherita would write off the list of Christmas presents in her mind. Unless she were to catch sight of that miniature jet plane, which can be piloted by means of two slender twenty-five-foot cables from the ground below, and it occurred to her that this might very well be the object of my long-suppressed desire. In which case, she would surely buy it.

That's Margherita's way, because she is so logically illogical. The fact that twenty-two years of life can be reckoned from one of my moustachios and twenty-two more from the other would never deter Margherita from buying me a toy jet plane.

Meanwhile it had grown late, and I had to take myself and my mountain of parcels home.

I got home, all right, and Christmas Eve went off as scheduled. Some day, when I write up 'my tragic youth', I may elaborate on the fact that instead of the usual Christmas cards I received an electric light bill, a bill for bottled gas, a *billet-doux* from the carpenter and other such sacrilegious nonsense. Thank God, everything turned out very well in the end; in fact, it was extremely touching. But I must return to the climactic moment, when the presents came into the story.

*

We went, in wedge formation, with the Duchess at our head, to the room where the Christmas tree stood. Presents were laid out all round the foot of the tree, every one marked with the recipient's name. Margherita got a great box, whose contents seemed to delight her. Then she asked abruptly:

'What about yours? Haven't you got one?'

'I don't know,' I answered. 'If you've given me what you promised, then it must be around here in one place or another.'

Sure enough, the Duchess ferreted out a parcel bearing my name.

'It's a present from her,' the Duchess explained.

Margherita was beside herself with curiosity.

'What have I given you?' she whispered.

'How do I know?' I replied. 'Let's open it and see.'

We opened the box, and there were a wonderful vest-pocket radio, a set of building blocks and a toy jet plane. I was overcome by such extravagance.

'How do you like them?' asked Margherita.

'Very much indeed!'

'Did I get what you like?'

'Absolutely! You hit the nail on the head!'

My friends stepped up, and the blocks and the plane caused them to evidence some surprise.

'Are those things for Giovannino?' they asked.

'Of course,' said Margherita. 'You can't understand,' she added, 'unless you know him the way I do. . . .'

The Duchess stretched out a tentative hand in the direction of the jet plane.

'No, it was given to me and *me* is going to keep it.' I said *me* and I meant it.

Now I knew why I was so happy over my presents, and I felt as light-hearted as if I had shed the forty-four years to be reckoned from my moustachios and returned to the same age as that of Albertino. Then I thought of the Giovannino of days gone by, who had never received a Christmas present, and I was sorry for myself, yes, very sorry.

'Giovannino,' I reflected. 'You'll never get anything out of life except what you earn by the sweat of your brow. And that's the greatest present God could possibly give you. May God be praised!'